Riding the Second Wave

Riding the Second Wave

How Feminism Changed Women's Psychology and Mine

Jessica Heriot Ph.D

ISBN-13: 9781548392154
ISBN-10: 1548392154
Library of Congress Control Number: 2017910295
CreateSpace Independent Publishing Platform
North Charleston, South Carolina

To My Mentors
Ruth Pancoast, LCSW-C
Len Press, LCSW-C
Jean Baker Miller, MD

Table of Contents

Poem	Revolution from the Inside Out	ix
Part One: The Personal is Political		**1**
	Introduction	3
One	Catching the Second Wave	6
Two	The Double Bind	12
Three	Motherless Daughters	23
Four	Body Politics	37
Part Two: Psychotherapy Is Political		**49**
Five	Getting to the Starting Gate	51
Six	Women Counseling Women	56
Seven	Practicing Feminist Therapy	67
Eight	Incest: The Last Box	81
Poem	In Memory of Anna	91
Nine	Finding a Therapeutic Home	93
Poem	Psychotherapy	115
Ten	Approaching Fifty	116
	Works Cited	121
	About the Author	129

Revolution from the Inside Out

It began with murmurs barely heard,
scratches behind a bedroom wall
causing fidgety sleep and restless days.

As whispers passed from mouth to mouth,
it could not be denied.
The air was thick with wrong.

A small consensus grew,
a core of shared meaning
carrying weight.

This gave them courage and they spoke their minds— gently at first,
hoping for understanding, asking the men to right the wrong.

A storm of derision and ridicule
sent them reeling,
backs to the wall.
Hands covered their noses,
concealed their eyes,
protection from the toxic fumes.

They came together,
spilled personal pains from overflowing buckets
of dashed hopes and opportunities lost,
shared the daily routine—
housework, orgasms, menstruation, and men,
vented resentments and simmering depressions.

They mentioned the unmentionable: crying terror of secret abortions
the shame of rape, the smashed eye, defiantly purple.

Some spoke of night-groping hands—
robber of innocence—
others of leering glances,
a quick grab of the ass
as the boss slid by,
making the workday a minefield in hell.

Word spread,
exploding in New York, Chicago, Boston, and Washington,
flowing like lava through Baltimore, St. Paul, and St. Louis,
seeping into the cornfields of Iowa,
turning the oldest oppression,
its lies and justifications,
to ashes.

From the faint murmurs of unnamed frustrations
to the most subversive coffee klatches ever,
in a "click" of pure understanding
women made a revolution
from the inside out.

Inspired by *In Our Time: Memoir of a Revolution,* by Susan Brownmiller (1999).

Part One
The Personal is Political

Introduction

Feminism: "To believe in the social, political, and economic equality of the sexes and to organize activity on behalf of women's rights and interests."

Merriam-Webster Dictionary, 11th edition

In 1968, I was a divorced woman and single mother, terrified of being alone, furious at my ex-husband for leaving me, and angry for having caused him to leave. Shorn of my identity as a wife (a role I clung to like a sloth to a branch), I felt like a displaced person. That's where I was when I found Women's Liberation in the winter of 1969. Though I had a part-time social work job—of only marginal interest—my identity was still rooted in the multiple roles of mother, wife, hostess, and creator of gourmet dinners. How many times could you sit in the park with other mothers of two-year-olds swapping recipes or chocolate mousse, an experience I distinctly remember. Pinned to the corner of a bulletin board at the University of Maryland School of Social Work was a small note announcing the next meeting of Baltimore Women's Liberation. The words leapt out, neon to my eyes. Furtively I wrote the information on the back of my hand.

On a rainy, bone-chilling February night in 1969, I knocked on the door. "Is this where the Women's"—lowering my voice—"Liberation meeting is?"

"No," said the woman who came to the door, baby in arms, "There's no meeting tonight. Someone must have put the wrong date on the note. I have some journals. Would you like to buy one?"

I went home with two issues of a magazine called *Women: A Journal of Liberation.* The faces of two young women looked out from the cover. Under their faces the word "WOMEN" was written in large block letters, a clenched fist filling the center of the letter *O*, mysterious and dangerous.

I honed in on an article called "Training the Woman to Know Her Place: The Power of the Non-Conscious Ideology." It began with quotations from the New Testament, a Jewish prayer, and the Koran.

"But suffer not a woman to teach, nor to usurp authority over the man, but to be in silence." (1 Tim. 2:12)

"Blessed art thou our Lord our God, king of the universe, that I was not born a woman." (Jewish Morning Prayer)

"Men are superior to women on account of the qualities in which God had given them preeminence." (The Koran)

This blatant display of woman hating astonished me, but what affected me most was what the authors said about the quotes. "The ideology expressed in these passages is not a relic of the past. It has been obscured by an egalitarian veneer. We are like the fish who is unaware that his environment is wet. Such is the nature of a nonconscious ideology."

That's me. I was one of the fish. In spite of my college education and a master's degree in social work, I'd never thought about having a career, and no one suggested I have one, except for teaching, that "something to fall back on, just in case." I had been expected to attend college, but my education was not considered a foundation on which to build a vocation. Rather, it was preparation for becoming a well-educated wife of a man on the rise, though this was never said directly in our progressive middle-class family. I graduated from college in 1962 with no career goal and no passionate interests or talents. Afraid to be alone, doubting my ability to make a life for myself, I decided, without deciding, to marry.

I didn't know on that February night in 1969 that my life would epitomize the prescient insight of the second wave women's movement—*the personal is political.* Feminism wove its way into my psyche, clarifying my relationships with my mother, father, and men in general. It untangled a psychological conundrum that had me tied in knots and informed every relevant issue from orgasms to motherhood.

I didn't know that psychotherapy and women's psychology were also political. As feminists began to uncover the patriarchal bias underpinning psychological theory about the female psyche, they saw its damaging effects on women's mental health. Feminism inspired me to become a psychotherapist and propelled me into a career-long immersion into women's psychology and feminist therapy.

Part one of this book is about the effects of feminism on my personal life. Part two is about the influence of a feminist perspective on psychotherapy and the psychology of women. In my journey to find a theory of practice, I describe the pros and cons of several theories of practice. I hope my thoughts about the essential ingredients for a healing therapy experience will offer some guidelines for those seeking help from psychotherapy.

The personal and professional overlap throughout the book, each influencing the other, but feminism is the melody to which the music always returns.

One

Catching the Second Wave

Housework is political. Abortion is political. Standards of feminine beauty are political. Women's oppression is political. Sexual Satisfaction is political. A reevaluation of male-female relations is political. What else are we on the verge of discovering? What other so-called trivial issues and private battles consigned to the "personal" will we bring to light and redefine as political.

Carol Hanisch (1970), *Notes from the Second Year*

I met Jim, who was to become my husband, while working as a secretary in the Psychology Department at Tufts University in Boston during the winter of 1959. He was six foot four with jet-black hair and gray-green eyes swimming in pools of dark circles. He had a loping gait and an easy, self-effacing confidence. We drank stingers at the Stafford Hotel, listened to jazz in dark clubs and smoky lounges, and heard Joan Baez sing at a bar in Cambridge. We drove to New Hampshire on snow-covered two-lane roads, his arm around my shoulder, a beer in his hand.

The summer after our winter fling, I had a job at the same summer camp as Jim. I was a counselor for a group of poor, mainly black twelve-year-old girls, and Jim was in charge of the "bad boys." He was drinking too much while I was eating mashed potatoes and cake and gaining weight.

During the next two and half years, Jim and I had what I would characterize as a regular on-and-off relationship. In one-off interval, I fell in love with someone who was not in love with me and with whom I would remain smitten for years. During my last year at Antioch College, Jim was back in the picture, driving the five hours through storms of snow from Lafayette, Indiana, where he was a graduate student at Purdue University, to Yellow Springs, Ohio. Spring came, and Jim wanted to get married. So, two and a half years after our Boston romance, I agreed. He wanted stability and a wife who would support him through graduate school and beyond. I wanted security, the identity marriage would provide, and an adult (that would be Jim) who would navigate the real world for me. I believe Jim was not aware of these unresolved needs I carried into the marriage, so good was I at feigning independence and self-confidence. How could this plan not backfire?

We married in New York City in August 1962. There was a reception, and my Antioch friends came. When the champagne took hold, my regrets rose to the surface and settled like lead in my stomach. I walked out of the reception, sat in a stairwell and cried.

The move to Lafayette, Indiana was a tough one, a sea change from the liberal little town of Yellow Springs, Ohio. Purdue was the state agricultural and engineering school, and at that time, Lafayette was far from your typical college town. There wasn't a café, bookstore, or art theater for miles, but the steaks were big and the corn on the cob, delicious.

One year later, we moved to Indianapolis, still a big cow town, but it had a real delicatessen, several jazz clubs, and rib joints. We made friends, and I was just beginning to feel comfortable in my first postmasters social work job when Jim's career took us to Baltimore. I remember my despair as we pulled into town on a dead-hot August day and drove up Pratt Street to Johns Hopkins Hospital, past blocks of decrepit housing. The cornfields of Indiana seemed like heaven.

As the years flipped by, I grew more fearful and unsure of myself, questioning my competence and judgment. I resented Jim's self-assurance, independence, and emotional aloofness, the very qualities I admired and had chosen him for. I resorted to sarcastic barbs and cold withdrawals, the only power I felt I had. His ongoing commentary about the physical attributes of random women kept my shaky confidence in my own attractiveness on tenterhooks. The fear of being alone kept me from leaving. I felt that my survival depended on keeping Jim bound to me.

In the fall of 1967, a year after my daughter, Anita, was born, my marriage was on a downhill slide, and a female friend of Jim's from work became a too-frequent visitor at our house. In 1968 the dissolution of our union paralleled the chaos of that notable year. On April 4, 1968, Martin Luther King Junior was shot. Jim cried, and my brother-in-law in the National Guard (who was living with us at the time) was trapped on the corner of Caroline and Broadway, the white-hot center of Baltimore's ensuing riot. In June, staring at the TV alone on our unmade bed, I watched as Bobby Kennedy was shot.

Jim was present in body but gone in heart and mind. He was obsessively building a frame for a sofa using a carved wooden banister railing for the back. I knew he was thinking about leaving and my anxiety was rising like floodwater in a hurricane. In August I watched the Chicago police beat up protesters at the Democratic National convention, but still I hoped. By October our marriage was over. It ended in a dark cocktail lounge after a last-ditch therapy session. Six years and one daughter later, Jim wanted a divorce; he didn't want to try. There was no going back. I hurled my wedding ring out of the car window and fell into a pit of self-blame. My pervasive dissatisfaction and resentment had driven him away.

Jim moved out. I had the sofa. His friendship with his coworker had blown into a hot romance. He got a job in Rochester, New York, and she went with him. I dwelled in a narrow band between desperation and righteous anger. My childhood terror of being helpless and alone emerged from the depths like the seventeen-year locusts. I found a therapist who pushed me through the post-separation period of fear, anger, confusion, and loss. One night he told me that he thought I had married someone (Jim) like my father. *Huh?* I was deeply offended and vigorously protested. Married my father? How trite. I'd had enough therapy and quit a couple of weeks later. On New Year's Eve at a lackluster party, I clinked glasses with a friend and toasted the demise of 1968. One month later I gobbled my way through the two women's journals that would change my life. I read about childcare, single mothers, abortion, and women's struggles to free themselves from the binds of their socialization. I was thirty.

On International Women's Day (March 8, 1969)—who knew there was such a day—I attended a Women's Liberation meeting and signed up for a consciousness-raising group (CR), the little tugboat that nudged this new wave of feminism into port. Each meeting had a topic: housework, motherhood, sex, marriage, work, appearance, femininity, relationships with men and women. Each topic was accompanied by questions. Are the jobs of mothering and homemaking fulfilling for you? How much equality exists in your marriage? Is your decision not to work outside the home one that you made, or did your husband and society make it for you? What is feminine? How were you trained to behave like a girl? Do other women threaten you, and why? Questions in 1969 that were wildly radical.

I can't recall specific moments from my CR experience when someone shared an incident that resonated to my core, but I do remember how each meeting uncovered the sexist underbelly of society's assumptions about women. I remember how connected I felt to the women in my group whose experiences mirrored mine, and I remember how empowered I felt as I said good-bye and walked to my car. It was a year of revelations—doors opening, curtains parting, fog lifting, well—used metaphors that described my own blown state of mind.

Women's liberation described those moments when the clouds of the "nonconscious ideology" parted and women saw with clarity how their personal lives were being dictated by society's socialization of women. These moments of insight were called "clicks." These were mine. I understood why I resented standing with the wives of graduate students as we chatted about nothing much while the men talked about work and psychology. I was also a graduate student along with another woman who was in the same psychology doctoral program as my husband, both of us hanging with the girls in the kitchen, our nonconscious acquiescence to our ordained role in the world. *Yikes.*

I understood my self-satisfaction when Jim told me that his friend, Lou, could not celebrate the success of his dissertation defense with us because his nagging wife would not let him. *Thank goodness I wasn't one of those harping bitches.* Not only did Lou's wife put him through graduate school while working full-time as a nurse but cared for their three kids, cooked, and kept house. I was ashamed of my false superiority and ignorant judgment of her character.

I understood how women's socialized roles went unquestioned when Jim's boss invited us for dinner. His wife, also a psychologist who worked beside him every day, made dinner, cleaned up, and put their five children to bed while her husband lounged in the living room, drinking wine and chatting with my husband. I barely saw her.

I understood how women were trained to view each other as competitors rather than friends when my friend, Sharon, wanted to introduce me to an acquaintance of hers, another divorced woman, who wanted nothing to do with me, seeing me not as a potential friend but as a competitor.

A breakthrough moment occurred as I stopped for gas on my way to a weekly seminar on feminist therapy. The attendant was filling the tank (the days before self-service) and began out of nowhere making racist remarks. Suppressing my socialized tendency to be nice, I said, "I didn't ask for your opinions. Just fill the tank." He shut up, and I had one of my first moments of empowerment.

I began to understand that my fears were not character flaws but a consequence of a lifetime of having internalizing society's assumptions about women. Divorce had kicked me into the world, and I was forced to confront my fears. Could I support my daughter and myself? Could I be alone? Could I negotiate the real world without a man? I decided that what was learned could be unlearned. This gave me hope and the desire to push on.

During the year that followed the breakup, I quit the deadly part-time job Jim had convinced me to take, traded the gas-guzzling Pontiac he'd got on a deal and had given me before he left, and I bought a stocky red Gremlin. I moved from the house we had shared during the last sad months of our marriage, rented an apartment in a leafy Baltimore neighborhood, and became a feminist.

Two

The Double Bind

Men experience no dichotomy between adulthood and manhood because the two are identical. It is impossible to be society's definition of a healthy woman and a healthy adult at the same time. A woman who tries to be a healthy adult does so at the expense of being a healthy woman.

Ruth Pancoast (1974), *Feminist Psychotherapy: A Method for Fighting the Social Control of Women*

That Was Then

I was introduced to the concept of the double bind in 1972 at the weekly meetings of the Washington D.C. mental-health collective where the seeds of feminist therapy were being cultivated. However, the first person to define the double bind was Gregory Bateson, an anthropologist and social scientist. In the 1950s, psychiatrists thought schizophrenia was caused by dysfunctional family dynamics, specifically the contradictory messages sent by parents, usually mothers.

The definition: A child is faced with two incompatible alternatives. A mother says, "Come hug me," but her body language and tone of voice give an opposite message. This creates a confusing dilemma in which neither choice is the right one. If the child heeds the command, he or she will experience the mother's cold rejection. If, on the other hand, the child does not do as commanded, he or she will feel guilty and confused.

The double bind could make someone crazy, which it does, but not in the way Bateson thought. What he didn't realize was that society had created a double bind for half the population, the female half.

The double-bind redux: Society conveys to women that they should find happiness and fulfillment in caring for and serving others, but at the same time asserting that they were not really valuable for doing this or should be more like men. Yet women who opt for independence over marriage or a career over motherhood, are considered anomalies and even condemned. Neither choice was the right one. The double bind.

In 1970, a clever and timely study sealed the deal. A group of psychologists, social workers, and psychiatrists were given a list of personality traits and asked to choose which ones best described a "mature, healthy, socially competent" man, woman, and a nongendered adult. According to these mental-health professionals, a "mature, healthy, socially competent" man shared the same traits as a nongendered adult. Both were described this way: "independent, active, logical, not easily influenced, adventurous, self-confident, and able to separate feelings from ideas."

A "mature, healthy, socially competent" woman was endowed with two sets of personality traits. On the one hand, she was described as "gentle, caring, warm, empathetic, and sensitive to the feelings of others." On a less positive note, she was also "passive, submissive, emotional, unadventurous, and unable to separate ideas from feelings." Ergo, a "mature, healthy, socially competent" woman looked more like an immature, unhealthy, socially incompetent adult.

We thought there were three bad options for coping with the double-bind dilemma. Most women, including my cohort of college-educated women, opted for the traditional tri-part role of wife, mother, and homemaker. A second option was to choose the male role by entering the workforce. Women who chose this path incorporated those qualities that were usually assigned to men: assertiveness, rationality, a willingness to take risks, and the ability "to separate feelings from ideas."

Then there was the third option. Women who wouldn't or couldn't choose between these two dichotomous options. I was one of those women. We tried to incorporate the positive female qualities spelled out by the mental-health professionals while holding onto our integrity as "mature, socially competent" adults. We wanted both, to be desired as women and to be respected as intelligent adults. In pursuit of the latter, fear of being seen as too confident and assertive, therefore unwomanly and undesirable, was a dark possibility to be avoided. On the other hand, it could be so easy to lose yourself in the art of pleasing that you could walk out on yourself and not even notice. Maintaining a balance between these two incompatible choices, adulthood or womanhood, could be exhausting. If I were too strident in my opinions, too firm in my perceptions, too direct in stating my needs or, heaven forbid, my wishes, I would be one of those pushy broads whom men seemed to find so unattractive. I did my best to be tactful, understanding, and supportive, the gold standard of womanhood, though enacting these behaviors often masked my honest opinions. Fear of being ignored or rejected contributed to my lack of authenticity. Most of all I didn't want to be perceived as emotionally needy. This I knew could drive a man away. At the same time, I was determined not to be defined by the familiar adjectives of female inadequacy. *No, I am not an emotional puddle. Yes, I can separate ideas from feelings, and solve problems. I can think.* The double bind drove me crazy, and I spent the better of twenty years of my adult life trying to resolve it.

Smoke Signals from the Home Front

It's in the nest of our families where we get our first and up-close view of male-female relations, and it is where I received those devilish double-bind messages. Even before my mother died, I'd made an association between out-of-control emotions and women. Dad was the placid Delaware Bay and my mother, the unpredictable ocean.

Though the pillow seals my ears, it is hard to block out the screaming punctuated by the sound of shattering dishes. I don't hear my father's voice and feel sorry for him because my mother is screaming at him. What, I wonder, has he done to make her so angry? Why is Mommy so unhappy?

Days later I am thankful when Mommy says, "Jessica, go tell your father dinner is ready."

"OK," I say, hoping this marks the beginning of the end of my mother's silent siege of anger at Daddy.

My mother was a fountain of emotions: joy, love, sadness, and anger—the emotion I feared. There was her red-hot anger, which could flare up suddenly, burning and stinging; and the ice-blue anger, bitter, freezing everything in sight. My father rarely got angry, and it seemed the better way to be. In my heart I knew I was more like my mother, a hotbed of feelings, inchoate and unexpressed.

When I was five we left New York City and moved to a Tudor-style house in Scarsdale, a thirty-minute ride by train or car to the city. In the 1940s, it was an all-American town of white, protestant republicans. My parents were Jewish, nonreligious and politically left of center. Margaret, my mother, was a Hungarian immigrant and embarrassed me in the most obvious of ways, her appearance. The other mothers wore knee-length skirts, nylon stockings, and brown and white pumps. They were crisp as crackers. My mother was as round as a fruit, wore long skirts and peasant blouses, and spoke with a Hungarian accent. Like other childhood outsiders, I was shy and afraid of being rejected. I felt that our little family in our too big house was like a ship detached from its moorings, adrift in a strange sea.

My mother died from cancer when I was ten, and her death solidified the messages I had already received about being female. My experience prior to and after her death, as I found out later, was typical. It began with secrecy. I knew Mom was sick because she wasn't able to visit me at summer camp. Only after I was mandated to remain at camp an extra week (fear of polio was the given reason) did I know her sickness was serious. As soon as I came home, I knew she was very ill. Her door was closed and stayed closed. Though I pleaded with my father to let me see her, I saw her only once, the day she died. Crying, I walked to her bedside. My mother had become a shadow of her former self, bone-thin, gaunt, and gray. She hugged me and asked about camp. The ordinariness of her question, "How was camp?" gave me hope. There would be other visits. Then she told me to go out and play. She died later that day as I was playing with the girl next door.

A few days later, what seemed like a party to me was in full swing in our backyard. I was confused. When everyone began leaving, I realized they were going to her funeral. I begged to go, but my father said no. After her death, her name was never uttered. Everyone around me supported this silence: my father, my aunts, teachers, and friends' parents. With no opportunity to say good-bye or grieve, I stifled my sadness, longing, and grief.

Dad was gone every night into the wee hours, leaving me with a housekeeper whom I named Fat Sue, who listened to the horse races all day while the afternoon sun illuminated a Milky Way of dust motes. I lay awake at night listening for the click of the key that turned the front door lock. Only then could I fall asleep. A new fear emerged, of being abandoned by the one parent left, my father. This was reinforced six months later after Dad married Hannah, my stepmother.

A couple of months after my mother's death, I sat on the steps leading to the dining room and overheard Dad's side of a telephone conversation. "I don't care what she thinks; I deserve a little happiness in my life." I understood that "she" meant me, and he was talking about Hannah, the nice lady who had paid attention to me. I knew then that my mother's anger and unhappiness had spoiled their marriage, and Dad was probably glad to be rid of her. Still, the idea that Dad might marry Hannah hadn't crossed my mind.

Over New Year's weekend, four months after my mother's death, I learned about their marriage from a family friend who tried to cushion my speechless shock by telling me that he too had a stepmother. "She was very nice," he said, "and I came to love her."

Dad, incapable of dealing with emotionally laden situations, afraid he would have to confront my crying heart, hadn't been able to bring himself to tell me about Mom's terminal illness, or permit me go to her funeral, or inform me about his forthcoming marriage.

I was determined not to be like my mother—unhappy, resentful, and angry, but containing these feelings was difficult. I had much to be angry about: my mother for dying and abandoning me and not permitting me to see to her; my father for not telling me how sick she was; not allowing me to go to her funeral; marrying Hannah in secret; delegating his friend (someone I hardly knew) to drop the news in my lap; and for having to be nice to Hannah, who was taking my mother's place. Outright anger was out of the question, so I squeezed the water from my anger until it was dry enough to hang on the line, a sheet of silent, cold, pouty withdrawal. After a few months of living with my hostile rebellion, Hannah decided she'd had enough.

I overheard her tell my father that she couldn't take it anymore. She was going to leave and walk to the train station. Overcome with terror, knowing this was my fault, I was sure my father would hate me. He too would leave and maybe not come home at all. It would be my own fault that I was alone with no one to take care of me. I rushed to their bedroom. Hannah stood in the bathroom combing her hair. Speaking in a small voice, I begged her not to leave. No response. I pleaded and asked if she loved me. Dad, his voice fat with disgust, said, "Jessica, don't beg." Hannah didn't answer, but looked satisfied. She stayed.

My anger was destructive. It had almost driven Hannah away. Desperate for love, I had begged her to stay, and this display of weakness had earned my father's contempt. I decided never to be that vulnerable again. I cultivated a facade of self-sufficiency and independence and prided myself on never crying. I was attracted to cool, aloof men who seemed to have everything under control and exuded a challenging elusiveness. But lurking in the back room lay my long-hidden fears. I worried that my unexpressed emotions would bubble to the surface and I, like my mother, would be too emotionally needy for a man to love.

Another source of home-front confusion: the women in Dad's life. It started with the war between Margaret, my mother, and Rebecca, Dad's mother. My mother's animosity was visible in a photo of my parents affectionately looking at each other across a jagged empty space where my grandmother's face had been scissored out. I never learned the exact cause of their war, but I do know the two women were cut from the same colorful cloth. Both were flamboyant, seductive, and emotional. Neither had more than a bare-bones education, but each thought of herself as cultured and avant-garde. Competition between the two women who loved my father was probably inevitable.

Grandma Rebecca considered herself a bohemian, a hostess to artists, Russian émigrés, and left-wing politicos, who gathered in the spacious first-floor apartment of her house on Barrow Street in Greenwich Village. I heard whispers about romantic liaisons and knew her long affair with a judge created havoc in the family for years. Dad never forgave her for the affair and disliked her flamboyance, her seductiveness, her penchant for melodrama, and for what he called her "pseudo-intellectualism." She dearly loved her favorite and only son, but Dad could barely conceal his antipathy toward her.

In my teens Grandma had moved to a one-room apartment on the third floor of her house on Barrow Street. Paintings hung haphazardly from ceiling to floor, and the air would be thick with the smell of roast chicken and potatoes. On our visits Hannah would lean over and kiss Grandma on the cheek. But as Grandma moved to hug my father, he would put out his right hand so she couldn't get through. Giving in, Grandma held out her right hand to meet his as her left hand reached to touch his shoulder.

My mother was also a woman who sought and attracted the attention of men. This was obvious from the photos in her three tattered albums. She is usually gazing into a man's eyes or leaning into him, his arm around her waist. There is a photo of her at a business dinner with my father and five other couples. The other wives are all suitably tailored, but my mother is wearing a white off-the-shoulder blouse and a white carnation in her hair. For all his disdain for Rebecca, Dad had married Margaret, a replica of his mother, with predictably dismal results.

Hannah, my stepmother, was an Israeli folk singer who had come to America on a tour sponsored by Hadassah, a Jewish women's organization. She was tall and stately, her blond hair swept up into a high bun. She favored soft wool skirts and silk blouses. In Rebecca's eyes Hannah was a more suitable wife for my father than Margaret had been. But beneath her sedate exterior, Hannah, like a volcano, could suddenly erupt. A mistress of emotional scenes and irrational outbursts, her anxiety affected all aspects of our lives. She was obsessed with cleanliness, and her thriftiness bordered on the miserly. Following Dad's example, I was cool to her hot temper, reasonable to her irrationality. I stayed out of her way and ignored her whenever I could. Dad's marriage to Hannah strengthened my identification with my father and, by extension, with men.

Another explicit and distressing lesson about women came from my father. Dad admired people whom he deemed "cultured" and "informed." By "cultured" he meant having an appreciation of the "arts," and by "informed" he meant having knowledge of current events and politics (preferably his own). He valued competence, rational thinking, and people (read men) who dwelled in the realm of ideas. "That Robert," he would say, "is a thinking person." Yet Dad was put off by informed, "thinking" women who voiced their opinions with determination and confidence. I never forgot Dad's reaction during a political discussion we had one day. I mentioned Bella Abzug, the famous hat-wearing liberal congresswoman who represented Manhattan from 1971 to 1977.

"I don't like her" was his immediate reaction. I found this hard to believe because his politics concurred with hers.

"Come on, Dad, you don't like Bella? How can you not like her?

"Ah, she's a pushy broad. She acts like a man." His voice was full of disgust, his hand shooing her away as he spoke.

I admit: Bella Abzug was brash, outspoken, and no beauty queen, but how her looks and lack of feminine decorum could decimate her credibility and render her point of view valueless was stupefying. There it was. The important women in his life, his mother and two wives, whom he found too emotional and viewed as his intellectual inferiors, were preferable to a smart, outspoken woman whose lack of femininity reduced her to irrelevance. This was deeply confusing and demoralizing. If being a woman meant being unable to think rationally or navigate in the world of ideas, I wanted no part of it. On the other hand, I didn't want to be seen as unfeminine, ergo, unattractive. Could a woman be smart and assertive and also desirable? Did she have to choose? I was barely aware that this was a question, much less a dilemma waiting in the wings to be identified.

The double bind began to unravel in 1972. I was thirty-three. Two years after my divorce, I had become involved in a relationship that had begun to chip away at my self-esteem. When we argued, his opinion of "what happened" cut a swath through my point of view, filling the cracks with self-doubt. He rebuffed my bids for affection, support, and understanding, reinforcing my fear that my needs were excessive. Yet I spent a lot of time trying to appease, support, and make him happy, to be the kind of woman men loved. I was afraid to assert myself, not only in the face of his judgments, but simply to separate my needs from his. I'm sure I was hoping that in time he would reveal a softer, gentler side, a willingness to connect emotionally, thus equalizing our relationship. I wanted to end the relationship, but every time I broached the subject of separation, a fierce panic set in and I would back down. My inability to extricate myself from this relationship drove me to psychotherapy.

Therapy began with unexpected questions about my mother that opened a trunk of unrecognized grief and a terror of abandonment. Therapy helped me make other connections. As a child I associated my mother (by extension myself) with unpredictable emotions and my father with calmness and restraint. After Mom's death, the unspoken injunction to suppress my grief, anger, and longing for love strengthened my nascent belief that having and expressing feelings were signs of weakness—the female kind. My father's choice of emotionally volatile women whose intellect he disparaged buttressed my scorn for women and boosted my identification with men. By being attracted to men who were alluringly aloof and cool, I was choosing the opposite of what I wanted. *Hmm.*

I learned from Len, my male therapist, that a man could "tolerate" my feelings and still respect me as a competent adult. He did more than tolerate my feelings; he welcomed and understood them. (Several of my friends and colleagues were in therapy with Len, and we joked about the many feminists he had in his caseload.)

While in therapy, I decided to write down all the words and phrases I associated with male and female. This is what I came up with. Male: reason, intellect, truth, control, sanity, father, men, good. Female: anger, sadness, wanting love, needy, overemotional, unhappy, mother, women, bad. *Wow.* I was shocked. I was a feminist with the same negative stereotypes about women as men. This was unacceptable. I consciously decided to change course. I promised to honor my need for support and affection, to stay tuned to the emotional melodies playing in the background, and to become better friends with my heart's desires.

Feminism identified the double bind. Psychotherapy helped me understand its origins, but the slim bombshell of a book, *Toward a New Psychology of Women*, by Dr. Jean Baker Miller clinched it. Dr. Miller was a small woman with graying hair who walked with a slight limp as a result of polio. Her firm, nonprovocative tone and carefully chosen words laid out a psychology of women and in the process unraveled the double bind.

She claimed that the character flaws assigned to women, weakness, vulnerability (defined as "need in the face of helplessness"), and the desire for emotional closeness (disparaged as dependency), were not flaws but feeling-states shared by all humans. Women have been the "carriers" of these feeling-states, allowing men to deny these emotions in themselves. *Yes.* This insight still carries the weight of truth today.

Women, as caretakers of the young and old, are in daily intimate contact with human vulnerability. This familiarity has made women less fearful and better able to tolerate these experiences. The ability to do this is a source of strength. *Bingo!* I had learned in therapy that knowing my fears, acknowledging my vulnerability, made me stronger.

By claiming that all humans, not just women, can feel scared, weak, and vulnerable, Miller created a wedge in society's view of women as inferior adults. By reframing women's knowledge of these feeling-states as a source of strength, she opened the door to self-respect. Women could value in themselves what had been considered the source of their inferiority.

After three years, I managed to extricate myself from the relationship that had driven me to therapy, enduring the panic any separation unleashed. Relief followed panic as my habits and wants reasserted themselves. The parts I had given away reassembled.

I kept trying to make my voice heard, fighting against the rules fed to girls with their juice and cereal—be nice, think of others first, be tactful, and this one from the Book of Common Knowledge: "Don't act too smart. You'll scare him away."

I had frequent misses. One of the most embarrassing occurred in a minicourse on feminist therapy I was teaching at Sheppard-Pratt, a private psychiatric hospital. The only man in the class made my life miserable by questioning everything I said, dominating class discussions, and raising irrelevant issues. Tactfully, I tried to answer his questions and politely endured his interruptions and non sequiturs, but I couldn't bring myself to confront his disruptive behavior. Not exactly a role model for the other women in the class, who also couldn't bring themselves to speak up.

Each time I stood my ground was a small victory, and after a time I stopped caring whether a man or men in general liked what I said or if they disagreed with my opinions. Eventually the double bind unraveled like a frayed rope. I became the person I am: logical, intuitive, rational, emotional, strong, vulnerable, tender, and tough.

Three

Motherless Daughters

On losing a mother: It's like coming home to find a hole in the ground where the house once stood, to look into the hole and ask "Where do I go now"?

Anna Quindlen (date and source unknown)

Mother

I can see myself cushioned in an overstuffed chair in a pea green, fluorescent-lit room. Across from me was Len Press, my therapist. Spinning in a circle of fear and confusion, I felt I had no center and wondered if I ever had one. I was thirty-three.

It was our third meeting when Len said, "Tell me about your mother." I recited the familiar facts: "She was born in Hungary and died of cancer when I was a kid. She and my father fought a lot. They had a lousy marriage."

"What else do you remember?"

"I can't think of anything."

"How old were you when she died?"

"Ten."

He looked puzzled. "I had the impression you were younger, three maybe. You know, ten-year olds remember a lot."

Caught short by his words, I was suddenly alert. After a moment, I said quietly, "I remember my mother taking care of me once when I was sick. She made me a sweet drink, seltzer water mixed with raspberry jam." Then like clouds, images floated by: my mother sitting at our metal kitchen table, doing dance exercises in her sunny bedroom, sitting on a white wooden chair in the backyard, legs crossed, her shapely calves disappearing into sturdy black shoes. I saw her large bosom, her deep purple lipstick and soft smile. I remembered the pretty clothes and the storybook dolls in their pink polka-dot boxes she couldn't resist buying for me. I was crying. *How can this be?* My mother had been dead for twenty-three years.

I met Len while working at the Kennedy-Kreiger Institute in Baltimore, the job I eventually left to become a therapist. He was the director of field education at the Maryland School of Social Work, and I was a field instructor at the institute. At our monthly meetings, I could see he was trying to convey some clinical concepts that were new to us and difficult to grasp, but his kind eyes and empathetic heart were as transparent as glass.

One day he paid a visit to the institute. He sat in on a conference about a new admission. The psychologist, the one who had invited Jim and me for dinner, whose wife was all but invisible during the visit, spoke first. Later Len expressed his shock at the coldness with which the psychologist presented the information about the child and his family as if they were objects, not people. It was one of those moments when someone says something you had sensed was true, but since your feelings had never been put into words, you didn't know you'd felt the same way yourself.

Margaret and Me

In therapy, I recounted all that had happened before, during, and after my mother's death. After rescuing her from the steerage, I realized that I knew very little about her and had a tangle of unanswered questions.

One summer evening in 1975, I found the courage to break the silence that had encased my mother. A soft gray light filled the living room. Dad, Hannah, and I were sitting quietly after dinner. I could see no smooth way to ease into this conversation, so I plunged in, "Dad, why haven't you ever talked to me about my mother?"

Silence.

Hannah said, "Yes, Leon, you should. I always said you should talk to Jessica about her mother."

My father looked bewildered.

"I want to know about my mother," I said.

"What do you want to know?"

"Why did we move to the suburbs? She hated it there, and so did I."

"It was her idea," he said. "She wanted to move."

I was stunned. I had always thought it was my father's idea. Why would my mother, a city lover, want to move to the suburbs? I absorbed the idea that she was the author of her own unhappiness. This information added to my long-held but reluctant suspicion that she was unbalanced in some way.

"Why didn't you tell me she was going to die?" I asked, desperation in my heart.

"She didn't want me to tell you. She didn't want anyone to know she had cancer. She made me go to different pharmacies so the druggist wouldn't know she was sick."

Oh dear, oh dear. What was wrong with that woman?

"But I loved her and wanted to say good-bye, and I wanted to go to the funeral, and you didn't let me, and no one ever talked about her again."

Hannah, quiet through all this, said in a thoughtful voice, "It's natural to want to know about your mother."

"Your mother was an unhappy woman. You remember how she wouldn't talk to you when she got angry? Do you remember that?"

Reluctantly, I said I did but resented his attempt to have me collude with him against my mother.

"I had to take her to New York to see a psychiatrist, someone who specialized in depression," he said. "But she loved you, Jessica. You were the center of her life. She was devoted to you."

Do you think I don't know that?

"I know she loved me," I said, indignant that he thought he had to tell me this. *I love and am loved by a crazy woman.*

Flesh of her flesh. I felt doomed. Sick-hearted, I knew more than I wanted to know.

Hannah rose and walked to the kitchen. "Jessica, would you like a cup of tea?"

"No, thank you."

I resigned myself to his assessment of Margaret as a depressed, neurotic woman.

Months later, perhaps a year after that disheartening conversation, I had an insight. Though I had been involved in the women's movement since 1969, I had not seen the obvious: Margaret, my mother, had been caught in the web of society's expectations of women in the postwar 1940s. A feminist version of my mother's unhappiness emerged.

By all appearances Margaret had achieved the American dream—marriage to a professional man on the rise, a queen in her suburban Tudor-style castle. Stuck in the house—she didn't drive—my mother was isolated and alone. She missed the stimulation and diversity of New York. My father, a decent but emotionally illiterate man, an up-and-comer, was gone all day and many evenings as well. These evenings, I later learned from a family friend, did not always involve work.

How could Margaret, a garment worker with an eighth-grade education, have left a successful husband and taken on the stigma of *divorced woman*? How would she have been able to support herself and a child? Trapped in a predicament with no viable solution, she became depressed and fought with the weapons of the powerless, impotent rage and silent, sullen withdrawal. I knew these behaviors well, having used them against my ex-husband when I too found myself caught in a marriage conceived in fear and hemmed in by societal expectations. A great weight was lifted from my heart. Margaret and I were now connected, not by our neurotic unhappiness but by the common bind we had both found ourselves in.

In 1969, twenty years after her death, I became what would have been inconceivable to Margaret, a single mother. Though single motherhood was still an outlier, the women's movement had my back.

"So, how do you feel about having a working mother?" the woman interviewing my daughter asked. Her interview was for an article in *Woman a Journal of Liberation* about children of single mothers. My nine-year-old daughter, Anita, offered this: "I'm glad my mom works because I think her job is important, not that she gets a billion dollars for it. She's a social worker."

One thing I never felt guilty about was working. I needed to work. In 1970 when Anita was four, I enrolled her in a co-op nursery school. All the mothers had to volunteer one morning a week. My morning was Friday, my day off. There was only one other single working mother. I was sure that the co-op mothers probably felt smug, safe in their young intact families, sorry for me swimming upstream alone. But I didn't feel sorry for myself. I was part of Women's Liberation, something larger, a movement that supported women regardless of their marital status. In fact I felt a tad superior to those stay-at-home moms whose lives I didn't envy. I don't know what the future had in store for them, but ten years later, the hurricane blew in. Many of Anita's friends' parents were divorcing. Homebound moms returned to the careers they were trained for, went back to or started college, took jobs, and began careers. By the eighties I was no longer an outlier but a pioneer.

I took my first writing class in the winter of 1995, with the goal of writing about the year of my mother's death. I titled it "My Tenth Year." This spurred me on to learn more about Margaret. I began to quiz anyone who knew her. My father's sisters, the most likely informants, were dead. When they were alive, I wasn't able to summon the courage to ask them for information because I knew they disliked my mother and blamed her, for what? I still don't know. Ten years earlier I had written to Elsa, my mother's sister, with a series of questions about Margaret, but never received a response. After my aunt died, my cousin found answers to my questions on torn slips of paper in the bottom of her dresser drawer and sent them to me.

Margaret Haberman was born in Hungary in a city named Munkác, pronounced "muncash." Elsa was already in the United States when my mother arrived at age fourteen. Their brother Robert came later. My mother lived for a while with Elsa in Buffalo but settled in New York City where she worked in the garment trades, training to be a dressmaker. My aunt's notes say she lived with a man but did not marry him. "Your mother was not promiscuous," her torn notes assured me.

Margaret wrote poetry and loved to dance, taking classes with Martha Graham, the mother of modern dance. An uncle told me that she was involved with leftist causes and met my father at a "do" on Thirteenth Street. "Margaret," my uncle said, "was a very modern young woman." A cousin and a family friend agreed that Margaret was vivacious and loved to have a good time.

I have many pictures of my mother in her teens and early twenties. She is often with young men, posing for the camera. At first, her hair is long and loose, flowing to her waist, and then bobbed, flapper style. There are photos of her at Coney Island and in Central Park. At a leftist camp in the Catskills, she faces forward, chin up, feet firmly planted on the ground, hands on hips. In photos with my father, she is rounder, full breasted and big hipped. They stand on the deck of an old steamship. My father is smiling, his arm around her shoulder. My mother is gazing up at him. They look happy. In the last photo I have of my mother, she is wearing a flowered dress and is gazing out of an open car window. She looks tired behind her cheerful smile.

I often perused the photos in the three tattered albums my mother kept and saw a sparkling young woman morph into a sad-eyed matron who died of cancer when she was forty-two, and I was ten.

My father never said where she was buried. But one day as we sped by, my father gestured toward the hillside overlooking the Taconic State Parkway and said, "Your mother is buried there." I never forgot the spot.

On a hot day in May, forty-seven years after her death, I visited my mother's grave for the first time. Her grave was easy to find. On a small flat stone was written, MARGARET KARCHMER, 1907 to 1949. This public evidence of her existence was deeply satisfying. I made some stabs at the hard grassy ground and abandoned the idea of planting a small begonia. Instead I placed it on top of the stone, a pot of pink begonias perched on her memory. I sat down next to her grave, amazed that I had actually come to this place. Absently, I brushed her stone clean, picking pieces of dried grass from the grooves between the letters.

"You have been waiting forty-seven years for this, haven't you?" I said out loud.

"I'm sorry. I'm sorry it took me so long."

I voiced my deepest hurt. "You should have told me you were sick. You were dying." Tears formed as I spoke. "You should have told me. You should have talked to me." Contrite. I should have come sooner.

I thought about telling her about my life and her granddaughter, but knew it wasn't necessary. *She knows everything. She has only been waiting for the day I will come. This visit is for me.* I wanted to stay longer but the heat was intense on this treeless hillside, and I was late for my next stop, the nursing home to see Hannah, the stepmother who came next.

Then I noticed. My mother's maiden name, Haberman, was missing. *How could that be? Don't they bury people with their full names? Where is the smiling young woman posing for the camera, the modern woman who danced with Martha Graham, who wrote poetry, and had a lover?*

My anger and sadness rose to the surface as I thought about the possibilities denied, her joie de vivre lost. On this testament to her existence, she is remembered only as Leon's wife, the last and least joyful part of her short life.

I reached into my purse for my soft-point black pen and drew a little triangle between Margaret and Karchmer, taking care to make the letters look like those on the gravestone, and centered her maiden name between Margaret and Karchmer.

Motherless Daughters

Like the colored blazes nailed to trees that point you in the right direction, so it was with my career. A tiny notice pinned to a bulletin board directed me to women's liberation; a handwritten sign on a white column introduced me to feminist therapy; and a little ad in the social-work newsletter led me to "motherless daughters." It read, "Looking for a female therapist to lead a support group for women who lost their mothers as children." *Yes. That's me.* I called the listed number and discovered a group called Motherless Daughters. Their home base was in New York City, but they had groups around the country. Lauren, the Baltimore contact, told me that Hope Edelman, author of the book, *Motherless Daughters,* would be speaking in Baltimore on Mother's Day, an event for women whose mothers died when they were children.

A surprisingly large group of women gathered in a sunny space above a local restaurant, a stroll from Baltimore's Inner Harbor. Hope

Edelman, thirty at the time, was tall and very slim, with the perfectly coordinated look of the suburban daughter she was. She spoke about her own experience as a seventeen-year-old girl and oldest child who was blown into adulthood after her mother's death. Her talk touched on all the themes and tender spots familiar to those of us whose mothers had died when we were young: lack of permission to grieve; the veil of silence surrounding our mothers' lives; the inability of fathers to parent and their not uncommon rush to remarry; our need for love and comfort; and our fear of asking for them.

After her speech we formed a circle and joined hands. Each of us said our mother's name, the cause of death, her age, and ours. "My name is Jessica Heriot. My mother's name was Margaret Haberman Karchmer. She died of cancer at forty-two. I was ten." Speaking my mother's name aloud in public was like bringing a part of myself, stored in the back of the closet, into the sunlit bedroom.

Edelman's book filled a gap by looking deeply into the web of effects a mother's death can have on a daughter during childhood and ever after. Right after the Mothers' Day event, I bought Edelman's book. Even now as I skim through the book, whole paragraphs leap out, and I am struck again by their pure truth. For example, this nugget: "The daughter who perceives herself as helpless and powerless against adversity is more likely to grow up fearing future loss. Instead of trusting her own ability to cope, she lives with an ongoing fear that another major loss will occur and she will collapse." My adult self didn't worry much about future losses, but separations could resurrect the panic of a long-gone ten-year-old. "Can I cope?" Edelman mentioned that at one of her talks she was asked what her biggest life challenge was. "I didn't have to think about it for long," she replied. "It's been learning to cope with separation and loss." *Yes, of course.*

I began leading support groups. The home office of Motherless Daughters had a perfectly sensible format for an eight-week group that hit all the important bases: abandonment, loss, fathers, siblings, stepmothers, intimate relationships, and motherhood. The women in my groups shared a legacy of loss familiar to my own: fear of being alone, of making changes, and taking risks. Others feared intimacy and commitment, of putting down roots, and always challenging themselves with new situations. Many cultivated a hard crust of toughness and independence. A woman in one of the groups, who had broken her ankle, dragged herself up three flights of stairs in spite of my offer to move the group to the first floor.

Nora, a therapy client as well as a support-group member, was eight when her mother died. Her father stopped coming home after work, waylaid at the bar until the wee hours, leaving her and her eleven-year-old sister to fend for themselves. After years of angry rebellion, failing grades, skipping school, and hanging out with all the wrong kids, she made a U-turn in her late teens. No task was too hard; no situation too difficult. Overcoming adversity with grit and tenacity had saved her and became her identity. From then on her pursuit to succeed was relentless. She whizzed through college and was on the road to a doctorate when she called me for an appointment. She was stuck, unable to complete her dissertation. Though there were some real-time obstacles in her path over which she had no control, she felt she should be working on her research. If she weren't so lazy, she would carve out more time to work on it. For Nora, this was a crisis of identity. Without dogged perseverance, she might become the failure that she, her father, and her teachers knew her to be.

Nora held on to her emotions like a poker player. She wanted nothing to do with the powerlessness, fear, and sadness she had felt after her mother's death and could not find compassion for the abandoned child she was. She dutifully called her father, visited once a year, and bore him neither ill will nor affection. But to her children, she gave her heart.

We don't think about losing a mother in childhood and its lifelong consequences as a feminist issue. In 1996, when I spoke about the consequences of mother-loss at a conference, I bemoaned the fact that the research only focused the effects on children failing to distinguish between mothers and fathers, as if the gender of the lost parent was inconsequential. More recently, I did find information about the outcomes of mothers' deaths on children in general, sex unspecified.

There are many variables that impact a daughter's response to her mother's death: age at the time of death, circumstances surrounding the death, permission to grieve, the stability of the environment afterwards. The gender of the motherless child matters. The women in my support groups claimed that they grieved at every life-defining event: college graduation, marriage, pregnancy, and birth of a first child. A mother defines for a daughter how to be a woman in important and superficial ways. Two motherless daughters I saw in my practice felt cheated because their mothers were not there to help them choose clothes (Does the dress fit? Does it look good?), apply makeup, cook (even the basics), set a table, or a write thank-you notes.

They remembered feeling isolated and ashamed among their "mothered" friends. To his credit, my father understood this and married Hannah, my stepmother, who provided those essential bits and pieces of feminine information.

Girls also have to deal with this new woman who is now both mother and father's wife. I resented Hannah who replaced the familiar living-room furniture (my mother's) with choices of her own. When she asked me if I liked the new furniture, I turned my back and walked away.

I was on the cusp of puberty when Dad married Hannah, an in-between age where I knew something and nothing about sex. Yet it felt like a betrayal that Hannah was sleeping in my mother's bed, that he saw her naked. Something sexual was going on, and I didn't like it.

The presenter for the Mother's Day event the following year (1997) couldn't make it, and Lauren asked me if I would speak. I was ready. I put together a narrative, accompanied with slides of photos about my mother's life and death and its impact on mine.

I spoke about my mother's love for me and mine for her, my lost memories, the secrecy shrouding her illness, the shock of her death, adults nudging me to forget and move on, my father's quick, secret marriage, and the velvet curtain of silence that rendered my mother invisible. I recounted that day in 1973 when I spoke about her death in therapy for the first time and my disappointment when Dad confirmed my fear that Margaret was depressed. I recounted my feminist revision of her unhappiness, my long delayed visit to her grave, and in 1995, my search for the facts of her life. On Mother's Day in 1997, I had the privilege of sharing my story of loss and reunion with women like myself, motherless daughters.

Margaret Redux

In 2011, I was looking through a folder labeled "Mother" when I saw the packet of photos with some notes written on the backs. Three years earlier I had employed a lawyer to draft a will who happened to be Hungarian. I asked if he knew someone who could translate the writing on the backs of the photos. He said he did. When the photos were returned I quickly read the words, noted that she seemed sad, and filed them away for three years. This time I read each note carefully, and a pattern emerged. On the back of the earliest photo, my mother at twenty-one, reveals: "My soul is so unbalanced it either cries or laughs...sheds tears or bursts out laughing, every minute, a new mood." In her midtwenties more despairing words, and in 1940, six months after my birth, she repeated the words she wrote at twenty-one and ended with, "I hope these unhappy nervous periods will soon pass." *Hmm.*

Could she have been suffering from a long-standing mood disorder? Maybe my father was right. During my thirties, struggling to shed the vestiges of my own female socialization and still unsure if, like my mother,

I had been the author of my own unhappiness, it was important that my mother not have a *mental problem*. Better to see her as a victim, a woman corralled by a sexist society. Sharing our common oppression had created a bond with my mother. Now at seventy-one I no longer needed to see her as a victim of patriarchal oppression.

Margaret may have suffered from a lifelong depression, perhaps the bipolar variety. Yet circumstances, the situations in which she found herself, could have coated her heart with despair. I didn't know what made her leave her family and country to come to America as a teenager. Was it a choice or an escape? How did Margaret carve out a life for herself in New York City at such a young age? Were there sacrifices? Recriminations? Did she regret moving to Scarsdale, the magic thirty miles that could keep her mother-in-law and Dad's sisters, who were at war with her, on the periphery of their lives? Did she know or guess my father was seeing other women?

Margaret left a mother, father, two sisters, three brothers, and multiple aunts, uncles, and cousins in Hungary. I have photos of both her parents. Her mother is standing in front of a concrete wall, hands on her hips, a kerchief wrapped around her head, wearing a shapeless skirt and blouse. Her father, standing on a concrete path, face forward, has no particular expression. He has a long, white beard is wearng a black suit and hat.

They were poor, and I knew Aunt Elsa sent clothes and money. Did Margaret write or send money? Did they write to her? Did she worry when Hungary entered an alliance with Germany in 1941 or when Germany invaded Hungary in March of 1944 and the deportations began? Did she suspect or know that Jews were being killed outright or sent to concentration camps? After the war, I can't begin to imagine her sorrow when she learned her family had died in a concentration camp. I have a vague memory of her telling me that a surviving cousin told her this news, but have no visual memory of that conversation.

I will never know the roots of my mother's pain, and it no longer matters. The only Margaret I knew was my mother. What I know for sure is that she loved me, and that's enough.

Margaret and Me

Four

Body Politics

It is very little to me to have the right to vote, to own property, etc., if I may not keep body and its uses in my absolute right.

Lucy Stone (1885)

When I was an adolescent the 1950s, the female body and its functions were unfit for public discourse. Teenage girls whispered about "the curse," their knowledge of its function opaque at best. Older women, hands cupped over their mouths, talked about going through "the change," an inevitable affliction awaiting all women. Female sexuality was a nonstarter. Freeing women from the bonds of society's strictures about women's bodies and sexuality is in my view the greatest contribution of the women's movement. The first two tales are about the bad old days. The last three are still relevant today.

Blood

I remember when the Women's Growth Center invited someone to speak about women's reproductive health. She arrived, speculum and mirror in hand. Off came her underpants as she demonstrated how to look at your vagina. *What?* It was all very shocking. I was thirty-three and had given birth to a daughter, yet the structure of the vagina and the female reproductive system remained vague. "Any volunteers?" she asked. I knew my feelings were outdated and ridiculous, but I was not ready for a close encounter with my vagina, tainted in my mind with blood and associated with shame.

My period arrived when I was twelve. Right on time. I was ready. One day as I was carrying a wrapped Kotex pad (as my stepmother had told me to do) to the trash bin, I met my father on the stairs.

"What's that in your hand?" he asked.

"My Kotex pad," I answered.

"That's disgusting. Don't carry that thing around."

I didn't know that men found periods revolting. I was drenched in shame and humiliation. I had a friend, Susan, whose father actually went to the store and bought Kotex for her. He must have been an exception. I believed my father. Menstruation should be kept secret from men—a dirty, bleeding secret that women kept from men.

My boyfriend and I were messing around in his dorm room. I was so tense I could hardly breathe. I had my period and was terrified he would find out. I pulled away. "What's wrong?" Silent, I couldn't tell him my secret.

"What the hell is the matter?"

In a small voice I said, "I have my period." He fell back on the bed, laughing.

"What's so funny?"

"You mean this is what you couldn't tell me? That's ridiculous."

A revelation. All men were not revolted by female bleeding.

My college roommate introduced me to Tampax.

"Where do you put it?" I asked.

"Put It where you pee."

Hum. I went into the bathroom and figured it out.

The inventor of the modern tampon, one Earle C. Haas, may his name be praised, invented the purse-worthy cardboard-covered tampon with its easy insert and exit. Good-bye to belts and pads, which always made me feel like a hospital patient with a urinary problem.

Though menstruation as a topic is well above ground, it can still arouse ridicule. While a candidate in an attempt to humiliate a female reporter during a debate, President Donald Trump said she was bleeding from her nose and from "you know where."

In my twenties I began to get headaches so bad that I went to a doctor, who told me I had migraines, a psychological problem. He prescribed Valium, which was, I thought, was for crazy people and never took it. By my thirties I knew the migraines were connected to my menstrual cycle. It defined my life. The week before my period was filled with rage and tears. Problems blew up like the giant balloons in the Thanksgiving Day parade. The rages receded when the bleeding came but were replaced by storms of brain-scrunching, immobilizing headaches. Two good weeks was what I counted on before the whole cycle began again. By the end of my forties the pre-bleeding days of feelings gone wild had subsided, but the headaches still made an appearance a day or two after my period ended. A few months before the last egg completed its journey and my uterus shed its lining, the crazies returned. *Enough already.* I was ready to see her go. My headaches disappeared with my periods. My diaphragm went out with the trash, and I no longer planned my life around my cycle.

The last person to comment on my menstrual cycle was a man. When I told my family doctor that I hadn't gotten my period for six months, he told me in an I-hate-to-break-the-news-to-you tone of voice, "The vagina dries and atrophies because it has no biological function anymore. You should consider hormone replacement." More shame. Shame to have it. Shame to lose it. Both men were wrong. I was excited to begin my monthly mimic of the moon and was glad to see her go.

Dr. Freud's Orgasms

In the Bad Girl/Good Girl era of the 1950s, sexuality was fraught with contradictions, apprehension, and ambivalence. In a prepubertal incident, my father caught me with my hands in my underpants and said I was being dirty, an early message that my vagina was a "no trespassing" zone. I didn't masturbate until my third year in college when my boyfriend, who couldn't believe I had not discovered this pleasure, told me what to do.

As a teenager, I remember bubbling with sexual urges, turned off at the source by a series of unpleasant experiences that drummed home the message "Boys don't respect girls who put out."

One message-heavy incident occurred on the lower deck of the ferry carrying me across the Great South Bay at night. I was making out with Richie, a handsome boy, desired by many. He drove me home from the ferry, kissed me good-bye, and said he'd call. I just knew he would. We had had such a good time. At a midwinter reunion party, he barely said "Hi."

I had another disheartening experience with a boy who claimed to like me though we were rarely together because he was always with a group of younger boys who looked up to him. He never tried to kiss or touch me. Finally on New Year's Eve, without a kiss at midnight, I must have said something. He said he respected me and did not want to do anything I didn't want. But I did want. I thought he also believed that the only kind of girl a boy could respect was one who doesn't want sex. It turned out he was gay.

An incident in my parents' apartment when I was sixteen put the final kibosh on my sexual urges. I was crazy about a boy named Mark, my first true love. Our relationship lasted a month, and he left me for Jennifer. *May she rot in hell.* I was making out with Mark in my bedroom when my parents came home and found us. My father took me aside and told me, "I don't ever want you in the house alone again with a boy." My love for Mark and our making out seemed pure to me, and my father's statement sullied it. I was doing something dirty; I was not a nice girl.

These few unpleasant sexual incidents were trivial compared to some of the truly dreadful stories women told me about their initiations into sex. But they impressed themselves on my psyche and shaped my ideas about women and sexuality. I crumbled under what I thought was the underlying message: Good girls don't want sex.

By college I was no longer interested, and my sexuality went underground and disappeared for years. It cautiously emerged after my daughter was born. After my divorce, in spite of my motto "When in doubt, don't," I had a lot of ho-hum sex. My orgasms were clitoral, usually by my own hand. I couldn't imagine having a purely vaginal orgasm.

Dr. Freud, a patriarchal man of his time, was wrong about everything when it came to women. He maintained that the "mature" female orgasm was vaginal. Clitoral orgasms were second tier, a prelude to the real thing. *Our Bodies Ourselves,* published in 1973 by the Boston Women's Health Collective (now in its ninth printing) broke the silence about women's bodies and made it clear: The clitoris is the queen of pleasure. Science caught up with myth when Masters and Johnson, having observed hundreds of women having sex and measuring their responses, concluded that the clitoris was the center of all female orgasms. What a relief for the scores of women laboring under the false assumption that they were sexual underachievers. I too was relieved to learn that the vaginal orgasm was a myth, having never been able to have one without clitoral stimulation. Then sometime during my late forties, in a long relationship with the man who is now my husband, I began having vaginal orgasms. What a surprise! They overtook the clitoral ones in frequency and intensity.

Now I don't think that Dr. Freud specified the age at which women should achieve the mature orgasm. Maybe "mature" orgasms are for "mature" women. Concerning the superiority of the vaginal orgasm, he was definitely right, though I hate to admit it.

Choice

When abortion was made legal in 1973, I couldn't understand what the fuss was all about. If a woman didn't want an abortion, she didn't have to have one. Apparently it was not so simple. The belief that all life begins at conception is impervious to argument. Antichoice forces have been able to chip away access to abortion, creating more stigma and shame to a choice that most women are loath to make and about which many are deeply ambivalent. Though abortion is legal, the topic is still as hot as burning coal.

I was one of five hundred thousand people (depending on who's counting) on a march for women's lives in Washington, D.C. on April 25, 2004. It was a nationwide gathering, a statement that most Americans support a woman's right to choose. I went with three other women, two of them good friends. I don't know what prompted the question, but it seemed appropriate. "So," I asked, "who's had an abortion?" Susan said yes immediately and the others followed. "I did." "So did I." The secret was out. All four of us had had an abortion; two of us had two.

My first abortion was a snap. In the pre–Roe v. Wade year of 1971, a friend put me in touch with an ob-gyn at Johns Hopkins Hospital where she worked. He said he would do it for nothing. Before abortion became legal, I needed to see a psychiatrist at the Free Clinic who would certify that my mental health could not tolerate the birth of a child. The donor was my new boyfriend on a night when I didn't bother to use in my diaphragm. Newly divorced, already a single mother of a four-year-old, I never doubted I would get an abortion.

I woke up from the procedure crying, sobbing really. The doctor said it was a reaction to the anesthetic. "Oh," I said, vaguely relieved. Up and around the same day, the recipient of copper-enamel earrings from my boyfriend, I felt fine. A blip on the screen. I never gave it a second thought. The doctor received a gift of his favorite bourbon, and that was that.

In 1974, I sat in the waiting room of Planned Parenthood with a handful of bored-looking teenage girls. Two weeks earlier, I had called and arranged a date. The proverbial clock was ticking. An only child, I had always wanted two children and felt ready to have another child, but I was already raising a daughter by myself, in an off and on relationship with a man who absolutely did not want to be a father. Having a child without the benefit of marriage was still unusual among middle-class women. Worries piled up. Could I be fired? Could I face colleagues, my parents, and the world as an unwed mother? The main problem: I wasn't sure who the father was. On vacation I had a marginal encounter with an old friend three days after the end of my period, muddying the genetic waters. The paternity issue stopped me in my tracks. I decided to have an abortion.

Time passed in slow motion. I felt pregnant: swelling breasts, pants and skirts that wouldn't button, nausea, and overwhelming exhaustion. A firm believer in a woman's right to choose, I hadn't given much thought to what this choice was about. It came to me one sunny afternoon in a lovely park by a stream lying on my back, feeling as fecund as the lushness around me, that short of war or mayhem, this might be the only time in my life when I would have to make a life or death decision.

The silence of the waiting room at Planned Parenthood was broken by a voice calling my name. I was taken to an examining room where the expected routine began: blood pressure, temperature, pulse, heart, diseases, allergies, and medications. Next, a brief description of the procedure and a once-over on birth control. Then the wait. The room was freezing. I moved from examining table to chair and back, pushing thoughts about the next step out of my mind.

Flat on the table, legs spread apart in the stirrups, a male doctor, in a green gown and mask stood at my feet, and a nurse was poised at my head. I started to cry right away. I heard a voice, practiced in soothing, say, "Now there's nothing to be afraid of. You'll hardly feel a thing." She was right. A prick of pain and a mildly uncomfortable stretching, scraping feeling inside. I was weeping, feeling myself plunge deeper and deeper into the heart of my grief. The world was centered in my body. Nothing else existed. I could hear the nurse's puzzlement. "Are you all right? What's the matter? Just relax."

"I'm as all right as I want to be," I answered. Then, sorry for my flip response, "I'm fine, thanks."

I cried through the whole procedure. Every few minutes, I could hear the nurse saying "Just relax" or "It will be over soon" or "Are you OK?"

I stopped answering.

In the examining room, I was given a blanket and told to rest. As time passed, I could feel my body returning to normal. The nausea and the yoke of fatigue, that slow cow-like feeling was gone. The litany of worries I carried was slipping away. I felt relieved.

In the waiting room where I had to stay for an hour, a suggestion box caught my eye. I asked for paper, found my pen, and wrote:

"I'm glad women have the right to choose, but having an abortion is not like getting a tooth pulled. I made an agonizing and unwanted choice. During the procedure, I wept for the life I was throwing away. The nurse saw my crying as a response to fear and pain and seemed unnerved by my emotions. I am not a teenager in need of soothing. I needed to mourn this death in peace. There are many responses to having an abortion. Some women must cry, not out of fear or pain, but out of a human response to loss and death. Taking a few minutes to talk with a woman about her feelings about the abortion will give a nurse the information she needs to be truly helpful."

I knew this had been my last chance. I would never have another child.

The hour passed. I walked out to protesters carrying signs. "Ban Abortion." "Did the baby have the right to choose?" *No, that choice was mine.* So who should make that choice, a woman or the state? It should be the women, who will bear, give birth, and raise the child or choose to put the child up for adoption (another brutal choice), but abortion is about death and needs to be treated with the gravity it deserves. I have never wavered in my support of a woman's right to choose abortion. Control over one's body is the bedrock of feminism.

The Eating Wheel

The objectification of women's bodies is an area in which feminism has made barely a dent. Though women have breached the walls of the president's cabinet, the Supreme Court, and the breathy heights of corporate mountains, a woman's face and body are still fair game for evaluation and judgment. Rarely is physical beauty a requirement for men.

Perhaps this will always be so, but it tells young women and girls that beauty trumps intelligence and competence, and that stinks.

One of the consequences of the obsession to be thin as a Project Runway model and fit as an Olympic athlete was a splurge of eating disorders: death-defying anorexia, the gorging and purging of bulimia, and the obsessive cycle of dieting and binging with its endless tallying of calories.

Women caught in the vicious cycle of dieting, losing weight, overeating, and gaining weight are like hamsters on a wheel, frantically running in place, and going nowhere. Anything can trigger a ride on what I call "the eating wheel": a goal to be the fittest girl on the swim team (true), or the wish to postpone the onset of womanhood. For feminist and author, Naomi Wolf, it was a glimpse into the future as she watched an older cousin looking in the mirror and disparaging her body. Becoming a woman meant having your body judged. Her anorexia began at thirteen, when in her own words, she "began consuming the caloric equivalent of the food energy available to the famine victims of the siege of Paris."

My turn on the wheel began when I was nineteen and held on until I was thirty-one. I was living in Chicago with other students from Antioch College on co-op jobs. Binging was all around me. My apartment mate was binging on things, filching small objects from the basement of the museum where she worked. A friend, Janet, was binging on food. "I bought you a half gallon of ice cream," she would confess, "but I ate it all." I needed to take control of something, and what could be easier than controlling what you put in your mouth. I desperately wanted to lose the ten pounds I had been carrying around through high school.

I had always worried about my size and weight. At sixteen my face was oval but my body was still chubby. I thought I was doomed to be like my mother and aunts, big breasted and wide-hipped? My plan was simple. I would eat no more than eight hundred calories a day. Calories were like money. I could spend them any way I wanted. If I blew six hundred calories on buttered biscuits for breakfast and chocolate-chip cookies for lunch, it was lettuce for dinner. I sunk to my all-time lowest poundage of 105. The cycle had begun. My obsession with food and weight clung on for ten years, as I rocked back and forth from thin to heavy, and from dieting to overeating.

When Jim left me, I surprised myself by not overeating to soothe my wounded heart and smarting pride. I lost weight without trying, a hint that maybe I could eat normally and maintain my weight. Cautiously I sampled from my trove of forbidden foods: raspberry coffee cake, French-fried potatoes, and blueberry pie. I still kept track of calories consumed but stopped counting every morsel I put in my mouth. I began to notice signs of hunger and fullness and tried to follow them. Then, almost without noticing it, I was eating normally.

Feeling satisfied with your body is an act of will for many women, so powerful is the multimedia blitz of thin, fit women. Many women never make peace with their bodies, though feminism has stood on the side of honoring womanly bodies whatever their size. It's a worthy goal even it takes a lifetime.

FYI: Two buttermilk biscuits with butter are 328 calories; three medium chocolate-chip cookies are 234 calories.

My Old Face

Our objectification of women has created a culture of female narcissism, a lifelong perpetual awareness of one's appearance. "Perhaps the most universal of gender-related beauty standards," says Gloria Steinem, "has to do with age." Middle-aged women fret about losing their appeal and old women are invisible. If aliens were to scan the contents of our magazines, television, movies, and the Internet, they would have to conclude that humans died young, so rare are old people present in the media. In 2013 the Census Bureau estimated that 14.51 percent of the US population is sixty years or older, but their representation in movies is paltry. People over sixty held only 11 percent of speaking roles in the hundred top films of 2015. For women, the situation is bleaker. A 2013 report from the Women's Media Center on the status of women in the

US media found that women over forty represented only 11 percent of female characters in lead roles.

My wise aunt had two mottos: "Old people are invisible," and "Vanity never dies." I did not grow up with women obsessed with appearance. Hannah, my stepmother, had great fashion sense and thought every woman could be attractive if she bought the right clothes, held herself erect, and was "femineen" (feminine with a Hebrew accent). From my aunts, messages about female attractiveness were definitely mixed. Neither aunt was overly concerned with her appearance. Although they liked clothes, they were not "shoppers." They admired intelligent women who were informed about politics, art, music, and books. Yet female beauty and fashion were constant topics of conversation. If the female stars of television and movies could have heard what my aunts had to say about them, they would have never left their dressing rooms.

Aunt Dora: "Look at her lips? Thin as a blade of grass."

Aunt Frances: "And squinty eyes." Frances scrunches her face. "She looks like a prune."

Beauty or brains? I split the difference. I didn't spend much money on clothes, didn't ride the crest of every fashion wave, but cared about my appearance. I used makeup but not too much and loved lipstick but didn't need to wear it all day. I wasn't one of those vain, shallow women who doted on their appearance and allowed their minds to gather dust

Then in my mid-fifties, I began to notice certain unwelcome changes in my face. I was more concerned about my looks than I had admitted. When I was sixty-two, I knew the jig was up. One summer on Cape Cod, in a sun-drenched cottage overlooking the bay, I obsessively glanced in the mirror or any other reflecting surface, not believing how old I looked. I cried, and was angry, then ashamed of myself for caring.

My song is every older woman's song as we are saturated with never-ending images of youth and beauty. When I began writing this book, I was seventy-four. I'm now seventy-seven, and sadly the shallow bowl of vanity still wars with the urn of graceful acceptance. My dear aunt was right. "Vanity never dies."

Part Two
Psychotherapy Is Political

Women's Growth Center collective
Baltimore, Maryland 1976

Five

Getting to the Starting Gate

Never take the path that has no heart in it. You can't lose if your heart is in your work, but you can't win if you heart is not in it.

Carlos Castaneda (from the A-Z Quotes website)

A good ten years before there was a women's liberation movement, I sensed that something was seriously amiss when it came to women. In a folder labeled "Feminist talks and essays" were two papers I had written in college. The first, written for a biology course at Antioch College in 1959, was titled "Male and Female Sexual Behavior: Psychological or Biological?" I wrote the second paper six months later in 1960 for a unit about women in America. From a carton of college essays, I had saved only these two.

In answer to the question posed in the first paper, I concluded that cultural and psychological factors played a greater role in women's arousal and responsiveness than they did in men's. *So far so good.* I went on to say that "Women's biological position is that of receptivity due to the nature of the process of intercourse" and that "her role in the sexual act is one of submission." (I can only assume this wad of sexual misinformation came from inexperience and the "experts" I consulted for the paper.) But all was not lost. I decided that if women were psychologically ready and cultural attitudes allowed them to be sexually responsive, women were as capable of sexual enjoyment as men. This paper was written before Masters and Johnson published their books on human sexuality.

The second paper was written for a class at the Merrill Palmer Institute in Detroit then a thriving city, where I spent an academic quarter in the fall of 1960. At Antioch College the "co-op" plan required students to alternate between studying and working. A biology or engineering major had few problems finding a relevant and interesting job. For an English major like myself, finding an interesting co-op job was not that easy, so I decided to go to the Merrill Palmer Institute. In 1960 the institute published a well-known journal on child development. It also offered a master's degree in psychotherapy and a program for undergraduates. I was one of a group of college students (all women) who attended the institute that fall.

We were required to take a course called "Core" where, to our disorientation and annoyance, we were informed that we had to devise our own curriculum. The teacher would be a resource, but he refused to tell us what to study. Much later, I came to see that "Core" was the perfect name for the course because its purpose was to encourage students to come to their own conclusions rather than blindly accept the opinions of teachers and other authorities.

The unit on women in American society, chosen by the group, was the inspiration for my paper on women's psychology. I wrote, "I immediately attached myself to Freudian psychoanalysis, which, for three days, seemed like the last word as an explanation of the female sex. Within a week I rejected it." I didn't want to identify with the picture of women painted by Helene Deutch, a psychoanalyst and "expert" on female psychology and sexuality, as constitutionally "feminine-passive." Nor did it seem right for women to be tagged with a "masculinity complex," for carving out a life of their own.

I was introduced to the humanist psychology of Abraham Maslow and Carl Rogers and met my first social workers, whom I liked and admired. By the end of the fall quarter, it was clear. I had chosen the wrong major, but it was too late to change my major to psychology if I planned to graduate at the appointed time. In the spring of 1961, I dropped out of college unable to write a paper on an obscure medieval playwright. No one was home when I opened the door to my parents' apartment. Of course, they were surprised to see me, and Dad with usual frankness made it clear. "Jess, what do you think you are going to do working at Woolworths? You can't even make the correct change." He had a point.

I returned to Antioch that fall, and slogged my way to the finish line, graduating in June, 1962. By then my starry love of psychology and social work had faded, so I hurled a hat at a graduate program in English literature at Purdue University where my soon-to-be husband was a graduate student. I threw a second hat at a master's program in social work at Indiana University (IU) in Indianapolis. Social work won when I received a government grant for tuition, books, and a monthly stipend. (The days when social work students received financial help to complete their master's degrees are long gone. Most of the students I taught at the University of Maryland in the 1990s juggled course work and their internships with full- or part-time employment.)

I began social work school that September. I'll never forget my first field placement at Indiana University Medical Center. Having never set foot in a hospital, to me the medical center was a maze of corridors, undecipherable medical records, and an army of fast-moving, white-coated people who all seemed to know what they were doing.

My supervisor told me to see Mr. X. on the ward. *What was I supposed to do?* Why was I at the bedside of this old man who lived alone, loved baseball, and whose lifelong job was delivering newspapers in a small Indiana town? He died two months after I began my weekly visits to his bedside. Had I been of any use to him, I wondered? I know now that my purpose was to ensure he received his local paper and be a friend, someone who cared enough to listen.

My second internship was at the Department of Welfare. I wasn't sure what my role was with the two clients assigned to me. Mostly I felt I was invading their privacy. My third internship was at a VA hospital. I had a no-nonsense supervisor who knew what he was doing and told me what to do. Best of all, I was paid.

When I began my training, social work embraced a theory called ego psychology, an outgrowth of psychoanalysis. Freud considered the ego, to be the mediator between the Id (our drives and impulses) and the realities of the external world. Ego psychology fit in well with the problem-solving orientation of social work. I was taught how to identify problems and the factors that impacted them, the resources needed and how to access them. Social workers mediated, interpreted, advocated, and facilitated—classic female roles—though I wasn't thinking in those terms at the time. Social workers also counseled patients' families. In the 1960s only psychiatrists conducted psychotherapy with patients. Today, according to the National Association of Social Worker (NASW), licensed clinical social workers provide 60 percent of psychotherapy services in America.

My first real job was at an in-patient unit for emotionally disturbed children at the University of Indiana Medical School. In the mental-health hierarchy at the time, psychiatry was at the top and just below was clinical psychology. Psychologists owned psychological testing, which made them feel important. A psychologist friend of mine who worked on the unit had the psychiatrists hanging on to his every interpretation of the psychological tests he administered to the new admissions. On the bottom rung were social workers, almost all women, who provided essential but devalued services, counseling families and connecting them with community resources.

On the children's unit, unusual at the time, social workers were expected to counsel patients, that is, the child patients. I was supposed to conduct play therapy. My social-work education did not cover play therapy nor was I given any on-the-job training about how to do it. This is amazing to me now. Did they think I would just catch on? I saw three latency-age boys and became proficient at making balsawood airplanes.

My last job, before I found my true career, was as the assistant director of social work at the Kennedy Kreiger Institute in Baltimore. I supervised social-work interns and had a caseload of families. I began the job in 1969, the same year I found women's liberation. With new eyes, I began to notice that mothers, the linchpins in their children's treatment, were the butt of blame when something went wrong: canceled or missed appointments, referrals ignored, or home-based treatment not carried out. A hallelujah chorus of maternal condemnation would rain down from the occupational and physical therapists, the behavioral psychologist, and the physician.

I was a single mother with many more resources than the mothers I saw. Yet even from my lucky perch, I understood their problems and hassles, their weariness and frustration all but invisible to the professionals. At interdisciplinary team meetings when it was my turn to speak, I tried to convey the context of their lives.

Physical therapist (PT): Where was Bobby last week? His mother didn't show again.

Me: Mrs. Brown missed Bobby's last appointment because she didn't have cab fare."

PT: She should have called and gotten a voucher.

Me: She thought she had enough money, but she was a dollar short. By then it was too late to get to the appointment on time.

PT: So, how about the bus?

Me: She could bring Bobby alone, but she says she can't manage with all three. Plus, she has to change buses.

Occupational therapist (OT): Can't she get a sitter? This is important for Bobby.

Me: She doesn't have family around, and as far as I can tell, she doesn't have friends in the neighborhood.

Physician: Well, see what you can do. Make sure she has cab fare next time. And is there money for a babysitter?

Me: I don't think so.

I knew that the field of developmental disabilities was not for me. This job, like the two before it, had fallen in my lap, unchosen. After I found feminism, I knew what I wanted to do. In June 1972, I left Kennedy-Kreiger without another job. I was not worried. My boyfriend, five-year-old daughter, Anita, and I hopped in my little red Gremlin and drove across the country. I knew what I wanted to do—counsel women.

Six

Women Counseling Women

The traditional therapist listens for pathology. The humanist therapist listens for self-awareness, the feminist therapist listens for the connections between the personal and political in women's stories.

Miriam Greenspan (1993), A New Approach to Women & Therapy

Women's Growth Center

At the Belvedere, then a crumbling queen of a hotel in Baltimore taken over by a counterculture fair, I saw this announcement tacked to an imposing white column: "Women in Mental Health Interested in Discussing the Impact of the Feminist Movement on Women's Psychology, Meet Here at 2:00 p.m."

A large middle-aged woman garbed in a brightly colored tent dress took command of the meeting. Her name was Ruth Pancoast. Ruth was a whirlpool of energy and self-assurance, and when she walked into a room, she was the main event. She had assembled a group of women from the Washington, DC area who were counseling women and developing theory about women's mental health from a feminist perspective.

At last, I thought, someone was thinking about how to apply feminism to women's psychology. My excitement was hard to contain.

Ruth made a point of informing me that she was already an experienced therapist, and it took several phone conversations for me to convince her to allow me to attend their weekly seminars, discussions that were on the road to becoming “Feminist Therapy.” Hungry to be part of these theory-making sessions, I made the round trip from Baltimore to Potomac, Maryland, every Sunday in 1971. Ruth was my introduction to a career-long immersion in feminist psychotherapy and the psychology of women.

She encouraged those of us from Baltimore who had gathered under her sign to form a feminist collective (a group of people sharing a common interest or purpose). Except for me—I had been a social worker for seven years—the group consisted of graduate students and newly minted professionals. After meeting together for about a year with no specific goal, Ruth nudged us into opening a counseling center for women where psychotherapy would be rooted in a feminist perspective. Tentatively we proceeded. We rented the first two floors of a tiny row house on a narrow street in a semi-hip Baltimore neighborhood, cleaned, painted, and scoured for used furniture. In February 1973 we nailed a sign to the front door: WOMEN’S GROWTH CENTER.

The Women’s Growth Center was one of several feminist counseling centers that opened their doors in the early 1970s: Women’s Mental Health collective in D.C. (1970), The Feminist Therapy Referral Center in Berkeley (1971), The Women’s Therapy Center in Philadelphia (1972), and Tapestry in Cambridge, Massachusetts (1976). All four are still in existence in some form.

A year after the growth center opened a whole new group of enthusiastic women joined the collective. Several members were in the process of becoming social workers, mental-health counselors, or family therapists. Other women were also welcome, and the group included an astrologer, photographer, community organizer, and a carpenter. We ranged in age from twenty-three to thirty-five, mainly white and middle-class. However, we were fortunate to have three African American women in the collective: Pam, a psychologist; Kay, a social worker, elegant and boundlessly curious, who joined the collective in her midfifties; and another woman who changed her name and left Baltimore for Hawaii. In those early days, African American women were rightly skeptical of the women's movement, a rebellion of white, college-educated women. Black women, from slavery forward, had always worked outside the home, so one could understand their confusion. How could well-cared-for women with nice houses and nothing to do but dust and mind the children be unhappy? One could understand their confusion.

Another problem was psychotherapy. In the minds of many African Americans, psychotherapy was for white people, and when black people sought therapy it was a sign of weakness. The stigma attached to having a mental problem came from comments like "Black women don't get depressed. They're the strongest people on earth." In her essay, "Mad Colored Woman: A Memoir of Manic Depression," Anne Taylor describes years of suffering before being diagnosed with bipolar disorder.

During the 1970s lesbians wanted visibility and a voice. Some feminists were not thrilled. Betty Friedan, the president of the National Organization for Women (NOW), famously called lesbians the "Lavender Menace." She thought being a lesbian was a personal not a political issue and that lesbians would compromise the credibility of the women's movement. In response, lesbians formed groups and published magazines that focused on their own liberation from societal oppression.

In the mid-1970s, it seemed that women were "coming out" all over the place. Women's liberation gave some women permission to embrace a sexual preference they'd been hiding in the proverbial "closet." Others gave loving women a trial run, attracted to the idea that a woman could better understand them than a man. A trial run became a long run for a few of my previously heterosexual friends.

Some women felt that being a lesbian was the truest form of women's liberation, precipitating a separation among Baltimore feminists. One Halloween, three apartments in the building where I was living threw a party. The gay women congregated in Sharon's apartment across the hall and the straight folks in mine. I knew many of the women at Sharon's and would go back and forth, uncomfortable about the whole scene. Now it's hardly worth a comment when a young woman announces she has a girlfriend, but in those days, it was huge. Though about half of the collective identified as lesbian, sexual orientation did not split the collective. I think our commitment to making the growth center succeed overrode our differences.

I can still visualize our meetings: a group of fifteen women scattered around the room, sitting cross-legged on used sofas, sunk into overstuffed chairs, or leaning on pillows propped against the wall. Decisions were made by consensus, a reaction to the top-down structure of the agencies and institutions where some of us worked and to society as a whole, where women's voices were either unheard or devalued. We truly wanted everyone to have her say, but it was a process that could make you want to chew nails. I had to keep myself from saying, "OK. We have gnawed this topic to the bone. I'm done. Let's take an old-fashioned vote." Yet somehow decisions were made and plans came to fruition.

I would like to say that our meetings consisted of meaty discussions about feminist applications to psychotherapy, but as a group of volunteers running a small agency, practical issues often stole the floor. Money was always tight. Our only source of income was fees from psychotherapy, and these were based on the ability to pay. I'm sure we saw some women for free. We debated whether to buy another sofa for the workshop room or a new fridge for the kitchen. There were more serious debates: how to divide the money we took in from therapy and workshops, and that ever-present unreachable itch, how to find a reliable source of funding.

Policy: A jar with a sign should be placed next to the coffee pot with a suggested donation so people would contribute but not feel embarrassed if they couldn't.

Financial salvation arrived in 1975 after congress passed the Federal Comprehensive Employment Training Act (CETA). The purpose of the bill was to provide jobs in public service for people who were unemployed. We desperately wanted a piece of that pie so we could hire collective members to staff the center. We applied and received CETA money and hired four collective members, each working part-time. We then had a person answering the phone, laying out and printing brochures, and paying the bills, all those tasks that make the wheels go around. The growth center expanded.

Between 1976 and 1980, in addition to individual and group psychotherapy, we offered a potpourri of growth-oriented workshops. A sampling: *Researching Our Matriarchal Past, Assertiveness Training, Taking Hold of Your Life, Motherhood: Past, Present, and Future.* The center also offered support groups to meet specific needs: women in the throes of separation and divorce, mothers without custody, and lesbians with children. I designed and taught a training course on feminist therapy for new collective members, mental-health professionals, and the just interested. With approval of the collective, a woman with an idea could facilitate a support group or design and lead a workshop.

I'm not sure how Dr. Miller met Ruth Pancoast. Perhaps she had heard Ruth speak and decided to ask her to present a paper at the 1974 American Orthopsychiatry Association conference in San Francisco. Ruth in turn asked me to be on a panel with representatives from the Boston, Philadelphia, and Berkley feminist mental-health collectives.

Having watched Ruth knead her thinking into a coherent theory of feminist psychotherapy, I was thrilled to hear her present her paper, provocatively titled "Feminist Psychotherapy: A Method for Fighting the Social Control of Women." I was amazed that our under-the-radar theorizing about woman-oriented psychotherapy had made it to a national conference.

Ruth's essay outlined the basic tenets of a feminist perspective. It began with four assumptions:

> First: Men and women are not equal. The power rests with men, who have kept women in a subservient position.
>
> Second: Men are encouraged to believe they are stronger, smarter, more objective and logical, therefore movers, shakers, and heads of households. They are also taught to keep their emotions to themselves, especially those telltale feelings that suggest vulnerability.
>
> Third: Women are socialized to believe that they are the weaker and less intelligent sex. They are trained through role modeling, overt and covert messages, nods and innuendo, to be gentle, tactful, accommodating, caring, and selfless. Women are

seen as naturally more passive, emotional, and vulnerable, therefore, predisposed to become mothers, wives, and homemakers.

Fourth: These assumptions created a double bind for women. The women, who had internalized the pink-wrapped package assigned to them, were caught in a tricky mind game. They had to reconcile society's belief that women's work— caring for men and children and keeping the fires burning at home— was not as valuable than the real work done by men? Even today, whether at home or on the job, caring for others is simply less valued. The solution, according to Ruth, was to encourage these "female-identified" women to develop their unexplored, untried, or defunct traditional "male" skills while helping them value the typical "female" skills they already had: household manager, logistic expert, director of finance, and psychologist—the one who knows without a word being spoken that Bobby had a bad day. However, women who identified with the adult/male role had another bad option for coping with the double bind. These women, still a minority, who chafed against the confines of female socialization, risked discrimination and humiliation for not being properly feminine women.

In 1978 the Women's Growth Center received a state grant to organize a conference on women and mental health. Five hundred women (if my memory is not exaggerating) attended from up and down the mid-Atlantic coast. The keynote speaker was Dr. Jean Miller. She had published *Toward a New Psychology of Women,* a book resonating with feminist therapists. I led a workshop on the double bind, a topic close to my conflicted heart.

Then in 1979 Dr. Miller graciously offered the growth center an opportunity to present a one-day workshop about feminist therapy at the American Orthopsychiatry meeting in Washington, DC. I was on a panel with three other collective members, and once again presented a paper on the double bind for women, which eventually became a chapter in a book, *Women Changing Therapy*. The room was packed; the excitement tangible. The only thing dampening our excitement was the meltdown at Three Mile Island in Harrisburg, Pennsylvania, just a couple of hours up the road.

There could be no doubt; feminism was seeping into the joints of psychiatry's brittle structure concerning women's psychology and their perceived mental maladies. At that point, feminist therapy was an idea just short of being adopted by the mainstream. Even the Maryland chapter of the American Psychiatric Association, noticing which way the wind was blowing, asked me to speak about feminist therapy.

The growth center had become everything I had hoped it would be. We had a strong group of women to carry on, so needing a break, I left the collective in 1979, six years after we'd nailed our sign to the door. I honed my skills as a therapist there and learned how to design and lead workshops and speak in public. I gave talks about women's sexuality, single motherhood, and, of course, feminist therapy. I also discovered that I loved teaching.

In 1981 the last CETA employee left, but a small group of therapists continued to provide low-cost feminist counseling for women. My last act with the growth center came in 1993. I and another former collective member persuaded the collective to sponsor a series of programs about women's mental health, psychology, and psychotherapy. For attending, social workers would receive continuing-education credits (CEUs), those golden nuggets needed to maintain a license to practice.

I eventually stopped following its fortunes, but just before moving to North Carolina in 2007, I was driving north on York Road, a long street that begins in poverty and ends with Nordstrom, when I spotted the growth center's iconic logo of a branching tree on a small sign in front of an inconspicuous building and gave it the thumbs-up.

I wondered if the Women's Growth Center, always on the edge of extinction, had survived. Then in May 2012, Jeannie, a former collective member, e-mailed me. Could I provide information about the center's founding for someone who was gathering information about feminist activity in Baltimore during the 1960s and 1970s? She also mentioned that the Women's Growth Center had a website. *Really?* Sure enough, there it was, with a lovely graphic of its emblematic tree.

I e-mailed them saying how pleased I was to see the center alive and well. A member named Susan responded and asked for my address. Then, sometime during the summer, I received an invitation to attend the fortieth anniversary and reunion of the growth center's founding, to take place on November 4th in Columbia, Maryland.

When someone asks, "How long have you lived here?" and you start calculating and cannot believe how long it's been, that's how I felt when I found out that the center had been in existence for forty years. *Wow.*

Another e-mail from Susan said they were trying to contact former collective members and anyone else who was affiliated with the growth center over the last forty years. I volunteered to find names and contact information for the women I knew. I provided them with a photo of our group, circa 1976, and copies of brochures I had kept that advertised our workshop programs. They asked me to forward a chronology of the first seven years and a shortened version of the narrative I had already written for this memoir.

I made reservations on a flight that touched down at the Baltimore-Washington Airport at 3:30 p.m.; an hour after the event was to start. Figuring the time it would take to get my rental car and not get lost, I would get to Columbia at about 4:30 p.m.

Frazzled and excited, I rang the doorbell. The door opened and a chorus of women screamed, "She's here. She's here." Overwhelmed, I was not sure what to do next. I pulled off my coat and gazed around the room. I spotted Lucky, with whom I organized the 1993 workshop series. I saw Eileen and Nancy, who had been collective members for twenty-six and twenty-seven years respectively; Levanah with whom I had designed and led a few intense workshops; and Katie, my old friend, at whose house I was spending the night.

After hugging old friends, I read part of the narrative that described the opening and first seven years of the Women's Growth Center and thanked the current collective for making this anniversary celebration possible.

Then from around the room, women described the center's ups and downs from 1995 to the present. I was awed at the persistence of each collective to keep the center going. The most heartening news of all was that the center was in the black, due in part (after much soul-searching, I'm sure) to raising their base rate for therapy to a big twenty-five dollars an hour. The growth center was now a setting for social-work interns who could see clients unable to pay the base rate. *Yes!* It was all over too quickly. Since I had come late, everyone had eaten and socialized before I arrived. But it was a soul-satisfying afternoon.

I couldn't have imagined that forty years after five women tentatively hung a sign on a row house door, the Women's Growth Center would still be offering low-cost feminist-oriented, counseling to women and their families in Baltimore City.

Pushing the Boundaries

In the 1970s second-wave feminists began finding their cumulative voice. Feminist newspapers, magazines, and journals (over seven hundred) cropped up around the country. In Baltimore, my home turf, the glossy magazine, *Women: A Journal of Liberation* published its first issue in 1969 and continued publishing the magazine until 1983. It evolved, as it did in many other places where women active in leftist groups and needing to find their own voices, separated from the men. When I asked one of the founders of Baltimore Women's Liberation what caused them to separate from the men, she said, "there were arguments between the men and women."

Services for women—rape crisis centers, battered-women's shelters, and mental-health centers—emerged in big cities and college towns. Baltimore was also a hotbed of feminist activity. Towson University in Baltimore County offered a program in Women's Studies in 1973, one of the first in the nation. The House of Ruth, a shelter for victims of spousal abuse, opened in 1977 and the Baltimore Rape Crisis Center in 1978. Baltimore, the pass-by city between Philadelphia and Washington, D.C. nurtured my feminist career. It was the perfect place to be. The city was big enough to have a lively women's community but not so big that I could be lost in the shuffle.

During this burst of feminist activism, psychologists, social workers, and mental-health counselors began questioning the conventional wisdom of psychology and psychiatry, noticing how it was mired in gender stereotypes and Freudian misconceptions. Feminism was beginning to infiltrate professional journals in articles such as: "The Early Origins of Envy and the Devaluation of Women: A Critique of Freudian Theory," by psychologist Harriet Lerner; "Kinder, Kuche, Kirche as Scientific Law: Psychology Constructs the Female," by Naomi Weisstein; and "The Psychological Consequences of Sexual Inequality," by feminist psychiatrist—an oxymoron in 1974—Dr. Jean Baker Miller. Miller's article drew a direct line between women's mental-health problems and their inferior standing in society.

A book that caught everyone's attention was *Women and Madness* by Phyllis Chesler, published in 1972. Uncovering psychiatry's pervasive male bias, she declared that the mental-health profession pathologized femininity. "Women…are hospitalized, predominantly for female behaviors: depression, suicide attempts, anxiety, paranoia, and promiscuity." Citing statistics from 1970 she brought attention to the fact that women were three times as likely as men to be diagnosed with the above symptoms as well as with lesbianism, (*true*), schizophrenia, and the mother of all female diagnoses, psychoneurosis (read anxiety and generalized unhappiness). Were women really sicker than men? Why were most psychiatric patients women and their therapists, men? The culprit, she claimed, was the patriarchal mental-health establishment blind to the socially sanctioned socialization of women.

I remember hearing her speak in a large, bare space on the second floor of a nondescript building in Manhattan. About fifty women sat on metal folding chairs. Full of righteous anger, Chesler indicted the psychiatric establishment for misogyny and fraud. I wondered about the small turnout. Maybe her sizzling critique of American psychiatry would be dismissed as too strident and fizzle out. It didn't, and her book eventually sold 2.5 million copies.

At this point, we thought that the majority of mental-health problems experienced by women were the result of inequality, female socialization, and the double bind. Feminist therapy was an antidote to the psychological maladies experienced by women as a result of their political oppression. A more comprehensive approach to women's mental health, psychology, and psychotherapy was to come.

Seven

Practicing Feminist Therapy

Feminist therapy concerns itself with the invisible and sometimes nonconscious ways in which patriarchy has become embedded... in our identities, our manners, and our experiences of personal power and powerlessness.

Laura Brown (1994), Subversive Dialogues: Theory in Feminist Therapy

In 1974, I accepted a position at Jewish Family Service (JFS). The office was located in the northwest section of the city, the heart of Baltimore's Jewish community. I was officially hired to fill a position in the division of services to the elderly but was promised referrals from the family division as well, which would give me the opportunity to do therapy.

I worked three days a week and had many extra days off for the Jewish holidays I hadn't known existed. My own religious education consisted of two years at the Reformed temple in Scarsdale, New York, where deciding what to wear and meeting boys were the highpoints of my short Jewish education. My mother, father, aunts, and uncles were "cultural Jews." Though they fully identified as Jewish, they had long rejected its formal practice.

For a single mother JFS was the perfect place to work. Occasionally I would ask if I could come in late because Anita had a cold or was participating in a school assembly. In an agency of Jewish mothers the answer was always, "Go home," or "You can't miss your daughter's assembly." Though JFS was warm and mother-friendly, it was definitely not feminist. The executive and clinical director were male though 90 percent of the social workers were women.

I had a small therapy caseload, almost all women. Most were deeply embedded in the tri-part role of wife-mother-homemaker with the same sad results. I saw Barbara who was pushed into marriage with a man from a well-known Jewish family by her status-seeking mother. After he left her for another for woman Barbara was devastated. Though she received ample alimony and her life continued to be comfortable, she was consumed with bitterness and was in constant competition with her husband for their children's affection. Barbara understood that she had succumbed to her mother's desire for her to marry "up" and that her status and identity had evaporated after her husband's desertion. Still young, she knew she needed to find another outlet for her restless energy, but as long as I knew her, she stayed stuck in regret and resentment.

I also saw a depressed single mother in her twenties, lonely and self-hating, desperate for a husband who could rescind her divorcee status and restore her to respectable, married motherhood. One woman in my caseload was afraid to leave her house, and another client was in therapy at her husband's insistence because she couldn't stop shopping.

I was a fan of the TV series *Mad Men,* that marvelous sociological slice of middle and upper class life during the 1960s when the stagnant waters of the 1950s were still clogging up the new decade. Betty Draper, the wife of adman Don Draper, was classic dissatisfied stay-at-home wife and mother. It took only a few episodes to see the seam of resentment just below the surface. She is a distracted mother, quick to anger, and low on empathy. While married to Don, whom she eventually divorces, Betty develops hand tremors, and since no physical cause can be found, her husband decides she should see a psychiatrist, who rarely speaks while Betty rambles on. Every so often her husband calls to ask about Betty's treatment. Each time the psychiatrist says something like "She is a very anxious woman, deeply disturbed, and needs further treatment." He assumes her tremors and anxious patterings are rooted in her disturbed female psyche rather than the stultifying situation she finds herself in. Had she found her way to my office at JFCS, she would have been a perfect candidate for feminist therapy.

At JFS I took my feminist perspective out for a trial run. What follows is pretty close to a typical first interview I would have had with Betty or any of the other women I described above. This session is with "Marcie," (not her real name) the woman referred for counseling by her husband because of her compulsive shopping.

Marcie comes in, and I stand and introduce myself. She tells me her name and sits down. I slide my chair to the side of the desk so it's not a bulky barrier between us. Sitting behind a desk endows one with automatic power and authority, the exact opposite of the message I wanted to convey.

"Is it OK if I call you Marcie? You can call me Jessica." She nods. "What brings you here today?"

Marcie doesn't hesitate. "My husband insisted I get therapy because he says I can't control my shopping."

"Do you agree?"

"I guess so. I see things I want, so I buy them."

"How do you pay for them?"

"I don't," she says. "I use my store credit cards, and when the bills arrive, my husband is furious. I don't blame him. I'm so ashamed. I don't know what's wrong with me." I don't address this statement. Instead I say, "So, tell me a bit about your life. For example, what's a typical day like?"

In a monotone voice, Marcie runs down her day from making breakfast for her two school-age children to putting them to bed.

"What do you like best about your day?"

She closes her eyes and smiles. "The peace and quiet after the children are in bed."

"Is that time you spend with your husband?"

"Not really. He works late and is so tired when he gets home. He eats the dinner I leave for him. Then he watches TV and goes to bed." *We'll talk about this later.*

"What don't you like about your day?"

Marcie answers right away. "The routine. Every day, the same thing."

"Are you saying it's boring?"

"Well…yes. But I can't complain. I have a nice house, two healthy children, and my husband takes good care of us."

I nod. "I understand, but you can still find your day boring."

"I guess so."

"You wouldn't be the first woman to discover that being a stay-at-home mom and homemaker isn't all it's cracked up to be."

Marcie smiles. "I'm glad I'm not the only woman in Baltimore County to find her day boring."

"What would make your life more interesting?"

"Well, shopping. Just kidding." She has a sense of humor, always a good sign.

"Did you work before you got married?"

"After high school, I worked at the Hecht Company (a department store) in the cosmetics department until I met Bill. We were married within a year. But in high school I was on the school paper and wanted to be a journalist. I wanted to go to college and major in journalism. My parents couldn't afford it, but mainly they were against me going to college. They thought it was a waste of time since I was going to get married, hopefully to a man who could support me."

"I understand. You did what was expected, followed the yellow brick road to marriage and children without actually choosing it. I did that too. For some women, it meant giving up a dream of doing something else like pursuing a career. In your case, being a journalist."

She is alert and attentive. "Do you still think of being a journalist?"

Sheepishly she admits, "Sometimes I write pretend articles about situations I see or know about."

"You can still go to college. Many women are returning to or starting college."

"Oh. How could I do that?"

"Well, that's something we can talk more about."

Can you find the feminist elements in the interview? Just kidding. When I said that she wasn't the only woman to find homemaking less than engaging, I was "universalizing" her situation, letting her know the problem was not hers alone. When I asked if she had worked before marrying, I was trying to find out if she ever had an interest or vocational dream that she discarded like used wrapping paper. Right away, Marcie cited her lost vision of becoming a journalist. Message: I am interested in who you are, beyond your marriage, your children, and the problem that brought you here. When I shared that I also walked into marriage without consciously choosing it, I became someone whom she could trust to understand her reality. If I had found a career, maybe she too could change her life path.

Today it may be hard to believe that these simple interventions were absolutely radical in the 1970s. For Marcie and women like her, feminist therapy was a light streaming through a crack between the floor and the door, a fragile hope that their lives could be different. By connecting women's personal problems to society's expectations of them, feminist therapy lifted the blight of self-blame and the dead weight of guilt. It bore a hole in a wall of resignation, and created an opening for self-awareness.

Psychotherapy and the Double Bind

The second option for coping with the double bind was to identify with the adult/male role. During the 1940s, 1950s, and most of the 1960s, these women were mainly "career women," a rare and unadmired breed. Married women worked only out of necessity like my two aunts, though my Aunt Frances confided that she hated quitting her job as a court reporter after her daughter was born. A mother who tried to keep her career alive was selfish. My mother agreed. "How can Mrs. Meyers (our neighbor and a lawyer) leave Gail every day to go to work? So selfish." It wasn't long before Mrs. M. raised the white flag of surrender and became a stay-at-home mother.

These women who navigated the male world were financially independent, and had incorporated those characteristics usually assigned to men: self-confidence, assertiveness, willingness to take risks, and the ability "to separate feelings from ideas." Often called "ball busters," or mannish, (read lesbian), they were deemed unattractive and undesirable. When I began practicing therapy in the midseventies, women who identified with the male role only sought therapy when their worlds came crashing around them. One example was Meg. After a long relationship crumbled, she sold her house and business and moved to a city where she knew no one. Undeterred, she was confident she would make it as she had during the many times she was forced to move from age six to seventeen. After a few months, her self-confidence shaken, feeling desperate, she returned to Baltimore and sought therapy.

As Meg recounted her multiple childhood abandonments, my expression of sadness and dismay took her by surprise. Tears formed. Meg woke up to the chaos that was her childhood and to the sadness, hurt, and disappointment that lurked beneath her mask of self-sufficiency. In response to these abrupt and unpredictable changes and the adults who couldn't be relied on or trusted, she had learned not to feel or need anything. Her rushed decision after the breakup of her relationship mimicked her childhood. Don't grieve. Don't feel. Start over.

Meg learned that while her ability to weather multiple abandonments had once served her well, keeping sadness and grief at bay, it was counterproductive in dealing with the demise of her relationship. She realized that attending to her feelings did not cause her brain to atrophy. This understanding facilitated a change in her attitude toward women. Meg shared the stereotypical view of women as overemotional and in need of a compensatory, rational, male mind. Once she grasped that her breakdown was caused by the dismissal of her emotions (the devalued female part of herself) she developed a greater respect for women. She joined a consciousness-raising group and became active in the feminist community in her town.

The double bind was a core issue for many women I counseled. They whittled away chunks of themselves and worried that their needs would drive their male partners away. Routines and habits were modified or abandoned, friendships ignored, and hobbies and interests left like pottery on the "unfinished" shelf. Statements like these were common: "I miss my little studio, but John is renovating his loft and really needs my help." Or "Bob loves his hiking friends, so I go on these outings, but it's not my thing and I feel like an outsider." Or "His video equipment is all over my place and I can't find a thing, but I understand how important this work is to him." These smart, competent women were effective and assertive at work, but with the men in their lives, they could deflate like punctured balloons.

Margo, more than any woman I counseled, was bound in the knot of the double bind. She was a baby boomer who came of age in the sixties and roared out of her Irish Catholic family and Baltimore row house into sex, drugs, rock and roll, philosophy, Zen, poetry, and the women's movement, which led her to me.

Her father, the venerated boss of the family, was considered the receptacle of knowledge. Margo's mother, whose virtues and beauty her father praised, was everything a "good woman" should be. A "saint," he called her. Margo adored and admired her mother, whom she described as modest, warm-hearted, thoughtful of others—especially men—never overtly angry, and ever ready to please. Margo learned that while society valued female virtues and cherished women "in their place," it valued men and all they stood for. She wanted a piece of the action, the freedom she thought men had—to be assertive and adventurous, to speak up, and put one's self first. Her socialization precluded it.

She feigned an attitude of carefree independence, earning the admiration of the "cool" carefree men she attached herself to. She wanted respect for her ideas and opinions but couldn't put them forth with clarity and conviction. Fear of hurting their feelings or being seen as brash and unfeminine held her back. She relied on her natural beauty and feminine graces, learned at her mother's knee, to keep a boyfriend tied to her. It was quite a juggling act, exhausting and demeaning, leaving her empty, resentful, and trapped.

Margo described a profound moment, an incident with her father that encapsulated all the confusing contradictions of the double bind. She and her Dad were having a discussion. Her mother was present but not speaking. She made a point her father could not refute. Satisfaction. Silence fell like a stage curtain. She saw his defeated expression. Guilt dissolved into shame. Good women don't challenge men; they protect and support them. In her desire to be seen by her father as an intelligent person, she had pursued her point like a man and won. Her father was no longer the all-knowing authority and she his perpetual student. She had lost by winning. Tears formed in the corners of her eyes and fell like pearls down her cheeks.

Her father could have acknowledged Margo's point, giving her the respect she craved. Doing that would have given her permission to exercise her intelligence without feeling she was diminishing him in the process. It would have helped Margo to see that it was OK to be an intelligent, assertive adult without sacrificing her desirability as a woman. But her father's ego and privileged place in the family would not allow him to do this.

After her mother died, she visited her father weekly and continued to pretend he was still the fount of knowledge, the last word on whatever subject he introduced. Though the visits were torturous and she resented playing the role of compliant student, the rules had been set a long time ago, and it was too late in the game to change them.

I had a long relationship with Margo and knew her in some ways better than I knew myself. To me she remains a perfect example of the crazy, mind-bending double bind for women.

Not only did the double bind make me crazy, but it could also corrupt therapy. In 1975, during my first year in private practice, a friend referred a couple to me. She hoped, as a feminist therapist, I could get them unstuck. The husband was a "been around" kind of guy with craggy good looks, older his than his wife. She was better educated, and social class was an issue lingering in the background. Though I empathized with his wife's plaintive pleas for recognition, her palpable neediness struck too close to home, and my attempts to help her give voice to her grievances were anemic. Instinctively I aligned with her husband, his calm, objective assessment of their problems, and his solutions to fix them. I told myself that I didn't want to alienate him by pointing out the validity of his wife's perspective. But truth be told, I wanted his admiration and approval. After three sessions, still stuck, they ended therapy. I knew I had done her a disservice by tacitly supporting her husband's cool-headed logic and knowing superiority, which undermined her need to be heard, feelings and all. This failure (countertransference in psychiatric terms) occurs when the therapist brings his/her unresolved issues into the therapy encounter. *Boo on me.*

Private Practice

While working at JFS, I was very active in the feminist community and counseling women at the Women's Growth Center. When I hung out my shingle in 1975, I was already known in the world of the Baltimore women's community as a feminist therapist. My first office was a sunny room separated from my living room by French doors with its own entrance from the front porch. The room had several incarnations. At first it was a "room of my own," a la Virginia Woolf, in an attempt to keep me from drowning in a relationship I couldn't sever. Then it became home to three different renters. I paid Anita, ten years old at the time, thirty-five cents an hour to answer the phone and to take messages. I bought a sofa, added two comfortable chairs, and commenced, as Malcolm Campbell says in his book, *Outliers,* to put in my "10,000 hours," the number of hours, required to be accomplished in one's field. I was a long way from accomplished. It took years of seeing clients to feel that I had a solid block of experience behind me.

I began with a few advantages. First of all, I really liked hearing people's stories and trying to figure out the sources of the problems that had brought them to therapy. Though many of my clients had lives very different from my own, empathy for their experiences and world views came easily. Leaning as I do to the informal, people quickly felt comfortable and with feminism in my pocket, I had a point of departure.

"Therapist transparency" was a key feminist concept I brought to therapy. Psychiatrists were perceived as having mysterious knowledge and magic techniques to cure people of their neuroses. Patients assumed that whatever the therapist was doing, he or she knew best. In reaction to this "father knows best" approach, I would explain to a client why, for example, I was asking about her first grade teacher or her mother's depression. As for my opinions…I set them afloat, trial balloons, and waited to see if one of them would be snatched and kept. Therapist transparency humanizes the therapist, decreases the inequality of the relationship, and promotes a collaborative relationship, facilitating trust.

One more plus. I was in therapy when I became a full-time therapist. I couldn't help but notice how Len, my therapist, related to me. I experienced the validating power of his focused attention. It was my first glimpse into the healing power of the psychotherapeutic relationship.

Len had an excellent memory for incidents and characters, but it was his ability to keep me on point when I wandered into the irrelevant brush that was truly impressive. I also have a good memory for the actors and dramas in people's lives. With practice I learned to follow a thematic stream and keep it from overflowing its banks.

Lucy: I felt so invisible. I had to leave.

Me: Like the party at your cousin's house where you felt out of place?

Lucy: When was that? Pause. Oh…how did you remember?

Me: It's my job. Consider me your memory.

My referrals came from women who found me through a friend or had heard me speak. Gay women wandered into my practice, not always for problems related to their sexual orientation. They came because they knew I wouldn't make it a problem. I met Pam only because her partner thought couples therapy might be a last-ditch effort to keep her from leaving. The problem, according to her partner, was Pam's emotional aloofness, her inability to be "intimate." I saw them for a few sessions until her partner called it quits, but Pam continued to see me.

Pam was slim and willowy with a stylish short haircut and tiny gold earrings in her pierced ears. She was funny, smart, gutsy, and savvy. Cool as a summer drink, with a barely contained ironic smile, she couldn't help being seductive, and I could see why many women found her attractive. Though Pam ran a tight emotional ship, one day she revealed something that was at the core of her identity. We were talking about sex, one of the problems between her and her ex-partner.

"I only like to make love to a partner; I never allow them to make love to me."

"Really? How come?"

"I don't like feeling vulnerable."

Hmm.

Would you like to talk about that?

"No."

I was never sure why Pam wanted to continue after her partner left therapy. There was nothing she particularly wanted to work on, and she didn't want to touch on her need to always "be on top." With little motivation to change, she wasn't in therapy for long. I didn't have the opportunity to explore her need to be on top and its psychological connection to being vulnerable, a typical response for "male-identified" women who wanted nothing to do with the stereotypical version of females as weak and powerless.

Soon I learned to ask my clients, "Tell me, what do you want from therapy?" We would go back and forth until we could agree on a set of goals. This is an important step both for therapists and clients. They are guideposts to keep therapy from getting stuck in the marsh, causing frustration for both. When I taught social-work students sixteen years later, I couldn't emphasize it enough.

The home-office arrangement was acceptable for a couple of years, but the confluence of work and home became too confusing. Doing laundry between sessions finally got to me. My first real office was in a once desirable apartment building located on Charles Street near Mount Vernon Park, a pleasant place for lunch on a sunny day. I shared the three-room apartment with two other therapists and saw many clients there. When I picture that office, one incident pops up.

The year was 1980. John Lennon had just been shot. The next day, I arrived at the office in time for my appointment with Linda.

"Hi, how are you?"

Though deeply unhappy, forever bemoaning her life, Linda was unable to express any true feelings. "How are you?" she asked.

Right away, tears began dripping down my cheeks. "I'm sorry. It just happened. Did you know someone shot John Lennon?"

She stared at me with complete astonishment. After a few moments of silence, she said, "You cried."

"You know, when something sad happens, it's not unusual to cry."

That moment did not provide an opportunity for Linda to feel and express even a little sadness about her lonely childhood. She was too scared of exposing any vulnerability, having grown up in a family where any feelings of sadness were unseen or dismissed.

Feminist therapists had long broken the rule of professional opaqueness in favor of appropriate self-disclosure. Yet, I wondered if I had gone too far in allowing my feelings to show. Later, with other clients, I came to realize that my honest expression of feelings was a permission slip, a green light, to be sad, angry, or to cry.

In 1980, I moved into a spacious office in another "seen better days" building. Six of us shared the rent. We met monthly to present and discuss cases and deal with "housekeeping" issues. Mainly we sat around and brainstormed names for a potential group practice that never happened. My favorite was Ace Therapists.

When I picture this office, I see Ava. I'm not suggesting that what follows is a way to forge a connection with a client, but it did create an instant bond.

I'd had migraine headaches since my early twenties and usually went to work anyway unless it was so bad I couldn't see. Even if I wasn't at my most insightful, I could be present and listen. This was a migraine day and my first interview was with Ava. I was holding a Coke can against my left eye trying to look casual about it. She sat down, took one look at me and said, "Do you have a migraine?"

"How did you know?"

"That's what I do. Hold a cold can of Diet Pepsi against my right temple."

We launched into a discussion of our migraines and before long were joking about our mutual torture.

Ava was in an amiable marriage, but a simmering doubt was bubbling to the surface and couldn't be suppressed. Was she attracted to women? How could she know if she was still married? It didn't seem fair to her husband. After a slow break from her marriage, she met a woman online and they became lovers and partners.

Since feminist therapy is based on listening to and honoring a woman's lived experiences rather than fitting those experiences into a prepackaged set of interventions, each client requires an approach that is specific to her needs. One size does not fit all. With Ava, a biologist, and a very rational, pragmatic person, I decided that I could be most helpful as an attentive listener, clarifier, and sounding board.

In 1985, two of my office mates purchased a three-story row house on Charles Street, just south of Johns Hopkins University. I chose a small room on the third floor. Soon women with histories of childhood sexual abuse found a path to my modest office. I think about a woman who was sexually molested by an older brother in a hidden corner of a dark basement. Her fear of elevators and parking garages (both of which she needed on the job) led her to therapy. There was Lucille, fondled as a small child by a favored uncle, a secret she held to her breast at great cost to herself, fearing the truth would break her mother's heart. Then came Beth, battling with alcohol abuse, who revealed three years of sexual abuse by a teacher in her Catholic school. Some women had histories so terrible that memories of their abuse were lost to their conscious awareness.

When my office mates sold the row house on Charles Street, I moved into my last office in a high-rise apartment building. By this point I had been in practice for twenty years, and I began to think of myself as "experienced."

Eight

Incest: The Last Box

The core experiences of psychological trauma are disempowerment and disconnection from others. Recovery therefore is based on the empowerment of the survivor and the creation of new connections.

Judith Herman (1992)

Survivors

As feminism was edging into the mainstream, who knew what would come next? Hallowed theories about women's roles and psychology were being questioned. Dark secrets, wrapped in silence—abortion, rape, and sexual harassment—were being revealed. Feminism was a nest of boxes, unwrap one and another box was waiting to be opened.

I don't remember the name of the first incest survivor I met. It was 1973, and I was counseling women at the Women's Growth Center. How she had the courage to tell me her secret in that dark age I don't know. The abuser was her father, a tyrannical head of house, who cowed her mother and sisters. Like most clinicians, I thought incest was restricted to a tiny percentage of the population, mainly those living in the Appalachian hills, where I now live. To my surprise, I was not shocked. I did not pull away. It was as if I had been waiting for someone to tell me this. In a classic light-bulb moment, I knew that she would not be the last. There would be more. In a society governed by patriarchy, with power in the hands of the father, who can if he chooses sexually abuse his children, I knew incest was a feminist issue.

The first book to view incest with a feminist lens was *Father Daughter Incest* by Judith Herman, published in 1981. The book supported my observation that incest families were most often rigidly patriarchal. The core of Herman's argument was that the existing theories—biological, anthropological, psychological, or biblical—that attempted to explain the universality of the incest taboo could not account for "the asymmetry in its violation." Fathers accounted for 94 percent of the perpetrators in her small sample of ninety families, supporting her idea that patriarchy, enforced in rule and tradition, accounted for this vast discrepancy between men and women abusers.

I was alert for signs of child sexual abuse, but it was three years before I saw my next incest survivor. Wanda was the oldest girl from a large family. Her father came to her bed, fondled her, and had intercourse with her from age five to ten. The abuse stopped after she got her period, a "blessing" she said. He then proceeded to molest all her sisters, one after another, right down the line. Like many other adult survivors, she was consumed with self-hate and a belief in her inner badness. "It is a wonder," Wanda wrote, "that I walk the streets and nobody knows I'm not normal." It took her weeks to begin to tell her story, most of which I learned from the letters she wrote to me and set down on the table in front of my chair.

"Do you want me to read them?" I asked.

"Yes, but don't read them out loud."

"May I ask questions?"

"I guess so."

I began to see more women whose childhoods were soiled by sexual violence. The fallout from the abuse, and its power to disrupt daily life, was usually the impetus for seeking therapy. Intrusive thoughts and memory fragments of the abuse can pop up anytime and obliterate an hour. For one woman whose stepfather molested her in the bathroom, taking a shower was an act of courage.

Doris was sexually molested by an older sister and exposed before age twelve to pornography. She learned how to perform like a porn star. Sex was for pleasing others, in this case, her boyfriend of several years. During sex she tuned out. Then her vaginal muscles refused to relax, and intercourse became too painful, a somatic symptom with an unmistakable message.

There are many ways to disconnect from painful or traumatic experiences: rationalization, denial, repression, and disassociation. We've all used one of these mechanisms in the course of our imperfect lives. Rationalization and denial were mine. Though I remembered everything about my mother's death and its aftermath, I shut off access to these memories, rationalizing that there was no need to think about the past. After all, it was a long time ago. I should be over it. As for my feelings, I tucked them away and denied their existence.

Disassociation was the method used by all the women I counseled who had experienced serious, ongoing sexual abuse. Clients described it as "leaving," "spacing out," or "going numb." Disassociation cuts off access to the terrible memories, but they make their presence known in the form of intrusive thoughts, nightmares, flashbacks, phobic reactions to specific situations, places, and objects, and unexplained bodily sensations. They are the road signs of trauma. The two women I saw in therapy, whose sexual abuse was ongoing, accompanied by violence and other acts of cruelty, invented entities who held memories of the abuse, unknown to the person herself. This is an extreme form of disassociation. Its diagnostic name is disassociative identity disorder (DID). Two of my colleagues were sure they were seeing a few clients with DID. I was skeptical. I had seen the movie *The Three Faces of Eve* and watched Joanne Woodward, who played Eve, transitioning among her three personalities. Multiple personality, like incest, was an anomaly, a rare occurrence, too "out there" to believe.

My skepticism dissolved after I met Donna. She had been hospitalized several times and had worn out more than one therapist. Our sessions were mainly silent, interspersed with her brief answers to my questions. I wondered what was going on. One day about three months after I began seeing her, I looked away for a minute, probably at the tree whose branches floated by my window. When I turned to face her, my eyes flew open. Sitting across from me was a three-year-old Donna. This large, tall woman was hunched over, thumb in her mouth, eyes glued to the floor. "Donna, what's going on?" No answer. "Are you OK?" No answer. "Donna," I said, "who are you?" A small, frightened voice answered, "I'm Ruthie."

I don't know if controversy about the existence of DID still exists. Once I had seen Donna, DID never stretched the boundary of my credibility. I could believe that unbearable traumatic events can be split off from conscious awareness and reside in the memory of the child who experienced them.

Doing this work was like walking into a dark room, stepping carefully to avoid tripping over obstacles as I groped for the perimeters. With help from Terry, a colleague who had seen DID clients, and lectures from the newly opened center for disassociative disorders at Sheppard Pratt Hospital, I learned how to proceed.

The purpose of therapy is to defang the traumatic incidents by bringing them into conscious awareness. For someone with DID, reliving her abusive experiences in the present quiets the child memory-keepers, who slowly become dispensable. The goal of treatment is integration, for the various "parts" to reside in one person. This is not always possible. A viable goal is for the person to be able to manage the alternate selves so they don't disrupt her life. A first step is to acknowledge and identify the various parts, a process usually met with resistance. Donna viewed two of her personalities, age seven and nine, memory-keepers of the worst abuse, with fear and disdain. They were the scared, helpless parts of her, and she wanted nothing to do with them. Her words: "They cry all the time and can't do anything right." The next step is for all the parts to know about and communicate with each other and the person herself. After Donna learned to trust me, a child part would emerge during a session and tell me about an incident. Having "spaced out" while she was talking to me, Donna would ask, "What happened?"

"Ruthie came out and told me about..." I would share the story with her. The memory would then be hers, which, of course, it was.

Donna and I worked together for four years. Understanding why she felt and behaved as she did was immensely helpful to her. She was better able to manage her child selves by acknowledging their presence and seeing them as parts of herself. However, occasionally a situation could arise, like a trip wire, resulting in the distortion of time and the loss of the trigger event itself. Occasionally she would indulge a desire by a child self to play with paper dolls or color with markers, activities that had been absent from her grim childhood. Donna was a profoundly decent person, who while in therapy, raised a son, worked full-time, and began putting together a career as an advocate for abused, abandoned, and orphaned children.

Feminist therapy was especially well suited to helping women who were sexually abused as children. Before a woman can tell her story and unearth painful memories, she needs to have emotional trust in her therapist. Every woman I saw with a history of sexual abuse wondered: *Will she believe or condemn me? Will she be repulsed by what I will have to tell her? Will she eject me outright from her office?* A survivor needed to know that I was unwaveringly on her side, that I understood the shame she harbored for failing to stop the abuse or her guilt for the acts she was forced to commit. I always placed the blame on the perpetrator, where it belonged. It is also essential that the survivor manage the pace of therapy. Feminists understood that a woman, having experienced only domination and powerlessness, had to be in charge of her own recovery. A therapist with her own agenda, pushing the client to retrieve memories she is not ready to deal with or prematurely urging her to confront the perpetrator, jeopardizes trust and blocks the path to healing before it can begin. Finally, the therapeutic relationship needs to be a collaborative one. A woman navigating this obstacle-strewn course needs a therapist who will be "with" her, a guide and a partner. Being "with" means feeling the sadness she's not ready to feel, mourning the losses she endured, and validating her sparks of righteous anger. This builds trust and the incentive to go on. A therapist who maintains a professional distance will have a more difficult time gaining trust, if she succeeds at all.

Anna was the most gentle of souls, an artist and protector of small animals, who had a long history of brutal sexual and physical abuse. She was coerced into doing some terrible things, which she could only communicate to me in writing. "Will God punish me?"

I wrote back, "I'm so, so, so, sorry you had to go through that. You had no control. You were forced. If so and so hadn't come into your life, this wouldn't have happened. God knows that."

Like many victims of childhood sexual abuse, she cut herself and abused drugs, mainly cocaine. For Anna, cutting was a temporary respite from the pain of her constantly intrusive memories as well as punishment for "acquiescing" to the abuse and other acts she was forced to perform. Anna, like Donna, struggled with demons from the past. Certain spaces, people, smells, or objects triggered flashbacks: taking a shower, blood, loud arguments, or sleeping in her bed could spark a flashback. Some days, just staying present was a chore and an accomplishment.

Anna and I had a contract. When she was reliving a disturbing memory and didn't want to continue, she would raise a hand, palm forward and we'd stop. My sessions with both women would often go past the therapy hour so I could make sure they were fully present when leaving my office. I saw Anna for about three and a half years. I knew a bridge had been crossed when a man, the husband of a good friend, came on to her in a car. She started "to leave" and felt the helpless child take over; but she caught herself, told him to stop, and cut off contact with him. A real breakthrough.

When her father came into some money, he gave Anna enough to finish college and complete her degree in art. We were both delighted. Then out of nowhere, she became ill, was admitted to the hospital, and died a few days later. I knew about her gastrointestinal problem but had no idea she was sick enough to die. I was overwhelmed with sadness and the cosmic unfairness of it. This intelligent, talented, tenderhearted woman was ready to take a giant step into her future. Then, boom, it was over. It was the worst day of my thirty-two years as a therapist.

Anna had given me a book of color photographs depicting the objects that were used in her abuse as well as a box made of frosted glass, the kind used in bathrooms to block vision. It opens from the top with a tiny wire hanger, a replica of the kind you get from the dry cleaner, sometimes used by adults to beat children. Today it sits on my bureau filled with marbles, a gift from another abuse survivor.

During a course I taught at University of Maryland School of Social Work entitled "Clinical Social Work Practice with Women," I passed around the book of color photos Anna had given me that metaphorically documented her abuse: a belt, a door with a lock, wrists tied with a rope, a mandala of multi-colored pills, and a hand with a razor at the wrist. The room was silent as students perused the book. Unable to hold back tears, I told them that Anna's future ended with her death at thirty-five.

I cared deeply about these women whose childhoods had been shattered and who were still standing. I hoped and cheered for them and was a willing anchor in their tumultuous lives.

By the time child sexual abuse had been identified in the mideighties as a serious, unrecognized problem, I had worked with survivors and had spoken to professionals who were being confronted with the terrible secrets of childhood molestation and rape.

Wanda, the abuse survivor who could only talk about her abuse in letters, reclaimed her dignity by refusing to attend her sister's wedding if their father, the perpetrator, was "giving her away." She also started a support group, "YANA, "You Are Not Alone," for women who had survived the dark nights and were yearning to repossess their lives. Wanda urged me to speak at a "Take Back the Night" rally. On a drizzly, damp, chill-to-the-bones Baltimore night, I stood on a makeshift stage and spoke:

"Of all the forms of violence against females, the sexual abuse of girls by a family member is the most damaging. It is the most devastating form of betrayal, the violation of the human contract to care for and protect one's children."

Mothers

The psychiatric community has had a long tradition of mother-blaming. Mothers were blamed for their sons' homosexuality, for schizophrenia (the double-bind messages that only mothers sent to their children), for being overprotective or not protective enough, and the final insult, failing to protect their daughters from incest. Psychiatrists trained in psychoanalysis thought mothers were the linchpins in the dynamics of incest families, unhappy, frigid, and emotionally cold. The outrageous implication was that their husbands, deprived of their conjugal rights, could be given a pass for using their daughters instead. An updated version of mother-blaming was advanced by family-systems theory. In this view, the family is a unit in which each member contributes to and has a role in its dynamics. The idea was that the mothers actively colluded with their husbands to maintain the family status quo and their protected place in the system. In the 1980s when I became interested in the role of mothers in incest families, these points of view were still prevalent. Though some mothers fall into this category, the assumption that mothers would knowingly permit the abuse to occur, failed to take into account the marital power imbalance that could contribute to their lack of protection. We expect mothers to protect their children, and it astounds and offends us when they don't. Anna's mother knew. "She walked in one night when he was abusing me. She asked him when he was coming to bed and left." I attended Anna's funeral. Someone pointed out her mother to me. It took all my professional restraint not to confront and shame her.

Passive denial was more the rule with my clients' mothers. They were intimidated by their controlling husbands and bound to them financially. A mother of a child whose husband forced their daughter to perform fellatio may not have known about this well-concealed abuse, but she tolerated her husband's humiliation of her daughter.

The road to my research about mothers began when I enrolled in the PhD program at the University of Maryland in 1983. The thought occurred to me that I might like to teach graduate students, and for that I needed a doctorate. The director of the PhD program at the University of Maryland School of Social Work was encouraging. All I had to do was pass the Miller Analogies test. I had a bleak history with standardized tests and worried I would do poorly on this one. No need, I did great. It turns out that social workers do very well in this test. I can see why, speaking as we often do, in metaphors and similes.

I had decided early on that I would use the doctoral program as an opportunity to explore issues relevant to women. In a terrible class about the role of institutions with the worst professor ever, I wrote a paper about the Women's Growth Center and the difficulties in sustaining a small nonprofit agency. In a course on group counseling, I wrote about the advantages of a peer-led support group for survivors of child sexual abuse. For Research 101, I designed a fuzzy and imperfect study about the role of mothers in incest families and put it on the shelf.

When it was dissertation time, I considered several topics, all of which seemed easier to pull off than my "mothers" project. On the plus side, in 1988 there was a paucity of empirical research on the role of mothers, so I figured the study might even make a contribution. In the midst of my ambivalence, I went to see my advisor. He said, "You need to think of your dissertation as a marriage. You're going to be together for a long time, so marry the one you love." That settled it. Mothers, it was.

Every week for eighteen months, I went to the old warehouse that housed Baltimore City Child Protective Services and read every substantiated case in which a family member had sexually abused a child. It was a long, detailed process. For someone like myself who operated in concepts and intuition, for whom statistics was a foreign language, and whose attention to detail was keeping track of appointments, conducting a research project was, in current speak, a "steep learning curve." To my surprise, I enjoyed it. I never looked beyond the next task, and eventually these tasks piled up and became a completed dissertation.

The question of the study was, Do mothers of children sexually abused by a family member or live-in boyfriend act to protect their children from further abuse? I studied 118 mothers of children whose sexual abuse was substantiated by child protective service (CPS) workers. A mother was considered "protective" if she separated from the perpetrator and was supportive of her abused child. Since I couldn't interview the mothers directly, caseworkers used a checklist to determine how supportive a mother was toward her abused child. Fifty-two percent of mothers were both supportive of their children and separated themselves from the perpetrator. An even greater number (seventy-two percent) believed their children's allegations, and most acted protectively (were both supportive and separated from the abuser). However, belief did not ensure a mother would be protective. About seven percent did not act protectively.

The data for my dissertation was collected in 1990 and 1991 and published in *The Journal of Interpersonal Violence* in 1996. Since then, there have been other studies about "maternal protectiveness." An article published in 2001, reviewing all the research about mothers to that date, found that the majority of mothers believed some or all of their children's reports of abuse. In another study, close to half of the mothers believed their children's allegations and acted to protect them from further abuse. However, twenty-seven percent were ambivalent. They believed that the abuse had occurred but failed to separate from or force the perpetrator to leave. Conversely, some mothers who did not believe the abuse had occurred were able to do just that. Understanding the factors that contribute to a mother's ambivalence is essential in order to know how to help her make the right choice for herself and her child—a further task for research and anyone who works with this group of mothers.

Feminism cut a permanent wedge in the hard rock of mother-blaming, and there is no doubt in my mind that it was instrumental in alerting professionals to what is now called "intrafamilial child sexual abuse." This happened because survivors told their stories to feminist therapists who understood the potential of a patriarchal culture to victimize girls and women.

In Memory of Anna

Who was there when you were dying?
Were the babies crying?
Were they scared?
Where was Stevie, only three,
a canary in the mine,
alert to danger in the air,
who loved to watch the planes take off
and made you late for work?

Where was Beth, a sturdy six,
whose cries, like white noise,
you barely noticed,
soothed at last when attention was paid?

Where was David, twelve and tough,
protective, and unpredictable?
Did he try to rip the tubes from your arm,
sass the doctors,
make a scene?

Did the One Who Waits
curled in the box you made for her—
who sent a fierce warning:
The World Is Not Safe
know something we did not?
Did she leap toward the light,
free from fear at last?

Was the Protector gone,
now that the babies were safe?
Was the Watcher watching,
mute as a shadow?

Where were the Doubles
who killed the cat?
Did they disappear when
they knew God saw their innocence?

Who was there when you were full of tubes,
strapped to the bed,
a mask clamped over your mouth,
silenced again?
Who was there when you died?
Did they all come together?
Did you die as one?

Nine

Finding a Therapeutic Home

Theory...gives us a base on which to organize what we do know. It brings some order to our practice by helping put into perspective the mass of facts, impressions, suppositions developed in the process of therapeutic contact with the individual.

Francis Turner (1996), *Interlocking Theoretical Approaches: Social Work Treatment*

Sampling the Therapeutic Landscape

Feminism led me to feminist therapy, which was essentially a political analysis of women's psychological ills from low-grade unhappiness to clinical depression, from generalized anxiety to agoraphobia. It described women's plight in the middle of the twentieth century when women (primarily white, middle-class and college educated) were corralled into marriage, motherhood, and homemaking. Reversing Cassius's advice to Brutus, feminism told women that the fault was not in themselves but in a society that denied them their full personhood. To the women I counseled at Jewish Family Services, feminist therapy was a beam of light pointing to land and the courage to alter their lives. Though feminist therapy continued to be my touchstone, I knew that I needed more than my feminist perspective to help women with complicated issues and intractable symptoms.

Two clients who needed more than my feminist perspective come to mind. Mary Ann, one of my first private clients, was so damaged by the narrow band of acceptability in the southern town where she grew up during the first part of the 1960s, that she was impervious to help. She was one of those people who could find an excuse to reject every suggestion and a reason to negate a kind word or genuine praise. I was so frustrated by her intractability, I wanted to shake her. I had not yet learned the value and skill of infinite patience.

Another client, Carol, had an insatiable need for love, or more precisely, to be mother-loved, and it hollowed out a hole in her heart that couldn't be filled. The third of four children, her mother seemed to have gone emotionally AWOL. Carol, a victim of benign neglect, was like a plant that despite the lack of regular watering survived but never thrived. Mothering for Carol was literal. It meant sitting in my lap with my arms wrapped around her. There were therapists, maybe there still are, who believe in reparenting. The idea is that the therapist provides a corrective to the client's deficient parenting. The person returns to her childhood to relive those times when comfort was withheld, self-expression stifled, feelings discounted, or the need for validation shot down.

What happened in the past is over. You can help someone face the past: feel sad, cry, punch a pillow, understand and manage its effects, but in my opinion it is arrogant to think you can redo someone's childhood. Therapist in loco parentis is ripe for abuse as I found out when the sister of a friend was being "reparented" by her therapist. This new mother turned out to be the authoritarian type, strict and demanding, controlling every aspect of her client's life. Sadly, this therapist was renting an office in the building where a group of us practiced. Shortly after my friend's sister had sued the therapist for malpractice, she left the building and may have had her license revoked. I hope so.

In Carol's mind nothing short of physical mothering could make a difference. I was supportive and emotionally available as her mother had not been, but for her the only way she could be made whole was for me to cuddle her. She never stopped being angry at my refusal to hold her. Though I assured her that I would never stop seeing her, she eventually ended therapy out of sheer frustration. I was always sad when a client quit because she felt I hadn't been helpful. But again and again I learned that you couldn't *make* people change if they don't want to. There has to be an opening, however small, that is receptive to change.

About ten years after I began practicing psychotherapy, I settled on a theory of practice, self-in-relation theory—an enlargement of feminist therapy, which coincided with what I had already been thinking and doing.

Over the years, I explored many theoretical approaches in my search to improve my understanding of behavior and my ability to help people with their problems. I will elaborate on four theories well known to both therapists and users of therapy: the "human-potential" movement therapies, cognitive-behavioral therapy, family-systems therapy, and of course, the daddy of them all, psychoanalytic theory. Each theoretical perspective has a point of view about human behavior, the causes of psychic suffering, and the therapeutic tools that mitigate problems. They all had ideas and strategies I liked and used in my practice but also drawbacks that kept me from getting on board with any one of them. In presenting these theories, their advantages and shortcomings, I hope that as potential or past consumers of psychotherapy, the reader will have a clearer understanding of these therapeutic approaches and understand the reasons for my finding a found a home in self-in-relation theory.

In 1975 when I opened my private practice, the human-potential movement was the new kid on the therapeutic block. It was a psychological breath of fresh air after decades of rooting around in the distant past with long, drawn-out psychotherapy. The theories born from this movement emphasized the present and were in contrast to the standard psychiatric treatment that searched for pathology. The humanist therapies focused on psychic health and personal growth. Psychological injuries could be excised in the here and now. Individuals could shed their defenses, attitudes, and false beliefs that blocked them from achieving their full potential. New therapies sprung up like spring flowers. Each had an overarching idea. If you could scream out your anger long enough (gestalt therapy or primal therapy), or find those places in your body where you held your sadness (bioenergetics), or be OK with your judgmental parents (transactional analysis), you would be cured, rid of the problems that hounded and confused you.

My first taste from this therapeutic buffet occurred in 1974 while I was working at JFS and seeing clients at the Women's Growth Center. I was leading a women's group and wanted to know more about group dynamics and, of course, myself. I attended a five-day workshop at the Humanist Institute in San Francisco, which promised both.

The story of my experience with the "humanists" is long and detailed, but in a nutshell, I became the group scapegoat. The reasons for this still remain a mystery. It began right away during the first group session when the leader began to berate me. A fierce panic overtook me. I felt like a kid again, the outsider, yearning for acceptance and afraid of being ostracized. A question pushed itself to the surface. *What would I do to belong?*

During the dinner break at the end of that upsetting day, I drove down to the San Francisco Bay. As I was watching the sun set fire to the sky, I had an insight, well a moment of pure clarity. *This has nothing to do with me. It's them. Something is wrong with them.* The intimidation continued during the evening session. Yet I decided to give the Humanists one more try. I had paid $200, a lot of money for me, and was not ready to call it a wash. During the following day I was benignly ignored, but in the evening a new leader took charge and the intimidation escalated. I quit the next day. My only regret is that I didn't demand my money back, something I would have surely done today.

I still can't figure what the "humanists" were about. Was the goal to intimidate people so they would eventually stand up and reclaim their dignity? It seems crazy even in those years of anything-goes therapy. However true to their brochure, I did learn about group dynamics, just not in the way I expected. I saw how the yearning to belong inflamed by an authoritarian leader and peer pressure could cause people to conform to bizarre group norms. To my great relief, I also discovered that I could trust my judgment and would not do anything to belong.

The so-called humanists were an extreme example, but many of these human-potential therapies were therapist-directed. The therapist knew what was wrong and exactly what you needed to do to overcome your "neurosis." If he, as it often was, suggested you to hit pillows and pretend that it was your mother or your boss, you did it without question. I had the same objection to this current flock of all-powerful therapists as I had had with the paternalistic psychiatrists who knew what was best for their female patients.

During a workshop I attended on gestalt therapy in Washington, DC, the two leaders, both men, were full of themselves and bantered back and forth about the group members. Still a nut for male approval, I wanted to appear cool and hoped they would notice me. They did, and I felt special. They were not so nice to a man whom I later felt they had humiliated.

There was another problem. The humanist therapies claimed to be gender neutral: that is, they applied equally to men and women. In truth, they often held the same stereotypical assumptions about women as traditional psychiatric therapy.

During a daylong workshop about transactional analysis (TA), a popular therapy in the late seventies whose mantra was "I'm OK. You're OK," one of the leaders cited an example of a woman who was very upset about being whistled at or called out to on the street. According to the leaders, this woman was not "OK" with her femininity. *Huh?* I raised my hand and said that it was not much fun being hassled on the street. Their facial expressions registered disapproval as in what's wrong with this woman? I could see they were surprised that someone had spoken up and disagreed with them.

Like psychoanalytic theory, the humanist therapies viewed each woman's psychological distress as her unique problem rather than the psychological consequences of inequality and social conditioning.

I did find some techniques from the human-potential therapies useful and stored them in my kit bag of interventions. For example, the technique from gestalt therapy of speaking the truth to someone—your father, your boss, or a lapsed friend—whom you imagine sitting across from you can be very informative. As a feminist who believed in therapist transparency and viewed the therapy relationship as a collaborative one, I knew that these strategies were only useful if they were presented as suggestions and endorsed by the client.

Behavior therapy has been around for a long time. In 1965 when I was a social worker on the children's psychiatric unit, behavior modification was used to manage the children's behavior on the ward. I admired its straightforward approach: identify the behavior to be changed, set up a program of positive and negative reinforcement, and, voila, behavior change. Success could be measured. I thought this was far superior to groping for meaning in the unsubstantial world of child play.

Two offshoots of behavior therapy became popular: rational-emotive therapy and cognitive-behavioral therapy. Both theories share the assumption that behavior is learned and can be modified. Our behavior is determined by our thoughts and beliefs. When a belief is rooted in misunderstanding, our attitudes, decisions, and behaviors, reflect that distortion. This creates anxiety, conflict, guilt, and other kinds of unhappiness. Bill is an example of a client for whom this approach seemed appropriate.

Bill was a social-work graduate student who sought therapy for anxiety and lack of self-confidence. The problem was that Bill strove for perfection and believed everything he did or achieved was second-rate. Niggling anxiety and a gnawing sense of inadequacy were his daily companions. "Have I read all possible references for the paper? Have I studied every shred of material that might be on the final?"

Uncovering the belief that underpins the problem is the first step. In Bill's family academic achievement was highly valued, and his father was the arbiter of excellence. Since his father neither praised Bill's good grades nor chastised him for the bad ones, he interpreted his father's absence of interest to mean that he was not good enough. If I were good enough, Bill thought, my father would surely tell me.

A second step is to contrast a held belief with reality. We compared Bill's belief that he wasn't good enough with the facts. In fact, he was an excellent student, and if memory serves me, had other achievements to his name. He realized that with no feedback from his father he had no idea what "good " was, let alone perfection.

The third step is to set a behavioral goal. Bill's task was to define "good" for himself. We started with study habits. How would he decide when he had studied enough? How could he determine when he had sufficient research for a paper? These questions launched us into a long, detailed conversation until he settled on criteria he could use to determine when enough was truly enough.

While these steps were helpful in creating some guidelines he could use to reduce his anxiety, the core of Bill's problem was his relationship with his father. It would take more than a well-planned strategy to tackle this complicated, emotionally loaded issue. Interpersonal problems loaded down with conflicting emotions, childhood fractures or traumas are not, in my opinion, so easily ameliorated with this approach.

Cognitive-behavioral theory is the "go to" therapy today. Putting one's belief to the test of logic or examining the feelings and attitudes that drive misguided thinking and behavior can be the right strategy at the right time. A few caveats: First, this process needs to be collaborative. A student in a class of mine who ordered her client to keep a journal of her thoughts was dismayed when her client came up with one excuse after another for failing to follow her therapist's prescription. Another problem for me was its de-emphasis on the emotional content that is often at the core of irrational beliefs, and in my opinion, needs to be dealt with directly. The theory, after all, is called cognitive-behavioral therapy, relying on our thought processes to think our way through the problems that plague us.

We all have families, so we know how influential they are in molding our beliefs and self-view. Family-systems therapy addresses the ways in which this occurs within the family. I admit that I've never sat down with a complete nuclear family: mother, father, plus two or more children. My opinion is that two people are a challenge, three, a crowd, and four or more, a camp bunk. A therapist who can sit in a room with a family and stay tuned into their emotions, reactions, and interpersonal dynamics has my total admiration. However, family therapy intrigued me, and I found that it could be useful with both couples and individuals.

The basic idea is that the family, like any other organization, is a system. If one member of the family has a problem, let's say an acting-out preadolescent boy, the whole family feels the effects, and their reactions in turn impact the person with the problem. Every family has its alliances ("my older sister and I always stick up for each other") and coalitions (two members who support each other). Most families have myths (grandma was a saint) and rules. Some are overt (what happens in the family stays in the family) and some are covert. In my family the covert rule was: We do not talk about my mother. This was never spoken. The pervasive silence said it all.

I remember when a client of mine popped up with this powerful but unspoken family rule: "Never talk about anything important and always be happy." How could she express her loneliness, her need for attention and love in a family where this was the rule?

Several theoretical approaches live under this umbrella, but facilitating harmonious family functioning is the overall goal. My big problem with family therapy was sexism. Early theorists simply ignored the fact that families, like individuals, were embedded in a patriarchal society. Women were often seen as the bad eggs in the carton, overprotective of their children, not protective enough, too emotionally demanding of their husbands, or too cold to touch. Wives were too needy; husbands too distant. The solution: wives should be less needy. "Pull back. You're putting too much pressure on him." The idea that husbands could learn to be more emotionally available was not in the playbook. Their worst idea was that mothers in families where incest had occurred were as culpable as their perpetrating husbands. In order to maintain family stability and their own place in the system, mothers "colluded" with the perpetrator to keep the abuse secret. *Yikes.* Eventually women family therapists, feeling the refreshing breeze of feminism, began writing articles and books condemning the male bias in family therapy and its stigmatizing assumptions about women. However, identifying family rules or myths, hauled unquestioned into a marriage or adulthood, can be useful in clarifying misunderstandings and lightening harsh judgments.

Though I had early on rejected Freud's view about female psychology, no hike through the therapeutic terrain can ignore psychoanalytic theory. Freud created a full-blown theory of human psychology, which was radical and innovative for its time. No one can deny that he had some game-changing ideas that are still relevant today, for example, the revolutionary idea that mental illness could be caused by negative childhood experiences. Another was the unconscious. It's hard to imagine any view of human psychology that doesn't give a nod to the unconscious. The concept of defense mechanisms—the many ways we stave off anxiety, an unpleasant truth, or a bitter reality—was a prescient insight. When a friend says, "Stop projecting" or "You're compensating for your lack of education," we know what she means.

However, Freud was an unquestioning member of the patriarchal society in which he lived, and he formulated a psychology of women that justified women's subservient position in society and pathologized those women who attempted to deviate from it. When women clinicians in the 1970s began questioning the chauvinistic views of psychoanalytic theory, every claim about female psychology was disputed. NO, female jealousy about not having a penis did not explain why some women wanted a life of their own. NO, women were not in perpetual competition with their mothers for their father's affection. NO, clitoral orgasms were only for the sexually immature. NO, the psychological problems women brought to therapy were not disorders of the mind but the results of social conditioning. NO, women did not need a fixer to get their psychological trains back on track. NO, women did not benefit from distant unresponsive therapists on whose blank page patients poured out their fears and unbidden desires. These victimizing and demeaning views of women were questioned and then discarded by the women clinicians who came of age during the second wave women's movement, opening a wedge for the development of a woman-centered psychology.

From social work, my home base, I had always lived with the motto, "Start where the client is," an idea more difficult in the doing than the saying. How easy it is to impose your idea about where to begin, dragging the client along to an unsatisfying end for both of you. Like every social-work student, I learned from the moment I laid my books on the desk, that "client self-determination" is sacrosanct. The client is the final arbiter of what road to follow and what decision to make. Finally, the apex of social-work values and its distinguishing feature is the idea of context. While other theories have focused on the intrapsychic life of the individual, social work has always viewed the person in the nexus of his family, neighborhood, and community, his ethnic traditions, religious beliefs, place on socioeconomic ladder, and, for some, the burden of racial and religious prejudice and discrimination.

Self-in-Relation: A Theory of Women's Psychology

The seeds for self-in-relation theory were planted in a book, T*oward a New Psychology of Women,* by Dr. Jean Baker Miller. In a chapter entitled "Ties to Others," she envisions a psychology based on women's lived experiences, encompassing both their concerns and strengths. "One central feature" she writes "is that women stay with, build on, and develop in a context of attachments and affiliations with others. Indeed, women's sense of self becomes very much organized around being able to make and then to maintain relational connections."

The next person to pick up on this theme was Carol Gilligan in her book, *In a Different Voice,* published in 1982. She was studying moral development in children with fellow Harvard psychologist Lawrence Kohlberg. The children in the study were given this moral dilemma. A man named Heinz has a wife who is sick and needs a drug he can't afford.

The children were asked, "Should Heinz steal the drug?" When Gilligan analyzed the responses, she noted that boys based their solutions on logic and fairness, what she called the "justice" approach. An example is Jake, an eleven-year-old boy. He thinks Heinz should steal the drug because human life is more important than the druggist's need for the money. If Heinz goes to jail, the judge should give him a light sentence because of the circumstances. The girls' solutions are based on what she called an "ethic of care and responsibility." This is Amy's response to the problem. Heinz shouldn't steal the drug. If he stole the drug, he might have to go jail and then his wife would get sicker and maybe die, and that would hurt a lot of people. He and his wife should talk it out and find another way (borrowing the money or getting a loan) to pay for the drug.

In Kohlberg's moral universe, the highest rung on the ladder of moral development is reached by logic and a full grasp of the concepts of justice and fairness. Less visible is the viewpoint that highlights the importance of relationships and an ethic of care, the reality of women's experience, a "different voice" at the moral table.

Throughout the 1980s, Dr. Miller and her colleagues at the Stone Center at Wellesley College had begun publishing a series of papers called "Works in Progress" that emerged in a book, *Women's Growth in Connection*, published in 1991. The papers taken together coalesced into a theory of women's psychology called self-in-relation theory. Like Gilligan's work, it emphasized the indispensable place of relationship in women's lives. I could relate. I've had deep, long-lasting friendships, and they have been a balm in the face of crisis and a bouquet in the face of joy. Like many women I've fretted about a misstep, a misinterpretation, some lack of attunement that could cause an irreparable disconnection. What did I do? What did she do? Whose fault was it? Even when I am not close to the person: a neighbor, an acquaintance, or as one friend dubbed it, an "activity partner," I knit my brows, and mull about what went wrong.

Another key idea is that women bring a set of skills to the relational table: the ability to empathize, to listen attentively, defer judgment, share one's related feelings and thoughts, to know when to offer comfort or support, and give criticism that doesn't sear the soul. Though women have used these abilities to enhance the development of others, especially men and children, Dr. Miller makes the point that when women employ these skills with each other, both people benefit from what she defines as "mutual empathy." But what exactly is empathy? Here are three definitions. For social worker Helen Harris Perlman, it involves "Feeling with and into another person, trying to understand how it feels to be you." Psychologist Carl Rogers agrees and adds that this should be done "without making judgments." Dr. Miller's definition begins by describing empathy as "a cognitive and emotional activity in which one person is able to experience the feelings and thoughts of another person" and adds another component. Not only does one empathize with another's experience but is "simultaneously able to know his/her different feelings and thoughts." For a therapist this is essential. She must be able to do both; convey her understanding of her client's emotional terrain as well as her own perception of that landscape.

In an article, "What Do We Mean by Relationships?" Miller dissects a conversation between two women, pinpointing those moments of connection and arrives at "the five good things" that flow from an empathy-enhanced relationship. They are self-worth, self-knowledge, zest, opportunity for action, and the search for other connections. The first two are obvious, but the idea that "zest" is a by-product of a mutually empathetic relationship is distinctive. By "zest," she means the energy, the sense of aliveness, the "high" we feel when we make an emotionally connection with another. "Opportunity for action," means that when one feels empowered to express him or herself within a relationship, (be it with a friend, parent, teacher, or therapist) it creates the possibility of expressing oneself in other relationships as well. If, on the other hand, one feels censored or misunderstood, his/her voice stifled, one can feel stuck or frozen. Then relationships are perceived as threatening rather than as sources of support and sustenance. Finally, relationships fueled by empathy create a desire for more connections, diminishing the sense that one is alone with his or her feelings and problems. When authentic expression occurs in therapy, it can function as a trial run, giving a client the courage to speak with honesty in his or her interactions with others.

To be present with interest and empathy, be it with a friend or with a client, is not usually seen as an activity. But it takes as much concentration as making a plane reservation online or wielding my little handsaw without nicking my finger (something I recently did). It is *doing* something. "Empathetic attunement," reframed as an activity, gives visibility and value to actions mostly taken by women, a skill that's often devalued and, at times, even punished. Two examples:

> Scenario One. A woman senses that her male partner is upset and preoccupied. She tentatively inquires, "Are you OK? You seem upset." He doesn't answer. But after a pause says, "Why do you always see something that's not there? Leave me alone." This woman may feel that her effort to create an opportunity for him to express his concern was wrong and that her effort to connect with him made it worse because he is now upset with her.
>
> Scenario Two. A woman notices her friend is upset and preoccupied. She inquires, "Are you OK? You seem upset?" Her friend responds, "Yes, thanks for asking, but I'm not ready to talk about it." Here the woman is rewarded for her empathic observation, though her friend, like her male partner, is not ready to talk about what's bothering her.

In the first scene, the woman's empathetic observation is rejected and perceived as an intrusion. In the second scene, her friend brings a willingness to engage, and the woman's caring response is understood and accepted. Each woman feels understood and, to grab an overused but accurate word, empowered.

Of course, women don't own the ability to empathize and other relational skills, but from an early age, girls are encouraged to develop them. According to Dr. Miller, girls come to feel that "picking up feelings of the other and attending to the interaction between them becomes an accepted and natural way of being and acting." My daughter knows immediately from my tone of voice as I pick up the phone and say "Hi" that something is amiss. Tentatively she asks, "So, how are you doing?" Recently, I had a serious misunderstanding with a friend. I called my husband and told him what happened. When I got home, he made no mention of the incident nor asked me how I was feeling. I'm pretty sure that a woman friend would have said, "Do you still feel bad about what happened with..."

Psychological Development

Everyone from Sigmund Freud onward seeking to determine how people develop psychologically has begun with the assumption that human infants are symbiotically attached to the mother with no sense of being separate from her. Development follows a course of gradual separation from the mother, which is seen as necessary for a person to become a self-sufficient, independent adult, which is the goal of psychological development. Psychologist Daniel Levinson who published his longitudinal study of men's lives, *The Seasons of a Man's Life,* in 1998, states, "When life begins, infants rely on their mothers to simply survive, however as they mature they become less dependent on others and increasingly self-sustaining...It ultimately prepares one for the onset and course of adulthood," that is, becoming "one's own man."

Psychologist Eric Erikson's well-known seven-stage theory of development assumes that a person (read man) must resolve his "identity crisis," that is, he must have acquired a firm sense of who he is before he can be ready for an intimate relationship. From a feminist perspective, his theory excludes the importance and need for relationships throughout the life cycle, and also ignores the various detours that more accurately describe the life courses of women.

Psychiatrist Daniel Stern, after mulling over reams of research about early infant development had another idea. He concluded that right from the get-go, infants experience themselves as separate beings and are able to distinguish themselves from their mothers. Though the boundary of a child's world expands, she/he always develops within the context of relationships. In his book *The Interpersonal World of the Infant,* Stern concludes that the goal of psychological development "is equally devoted to the seeking and creating of inter-subjective union with another." When a baby shakes a rattle and hears the noise, the baby smiles. The mother smiles back. This tells the infant that the mother sees and approves of her child's enjoyment. The infant reciprocates with a bigger smile, letting the mother know that the she or he has received her message. Voila, mutual empathy.

What would a theory of human psychological developmental look like if it included the importance of and the ability to establish and maintain relationships? What if the relational skills traditionally assigned to women were also considered hallmarks of adult development? Perhaps men as well as women would be actively involved in the nurture and care of others. Perhaps boys as well as girls would be schooled in the relational arts.

Exploring this relational terrain is a book, *The Space Between Us* by Ruth Ellen Josselson. She describes the kinds of relationships people need at different life stages. For example, the relational need of an infant is for "holding." We have all seen images of infants deprived of human touch, motionless and blank-eyed in their cribs. Each form of relationship has its opposite. Too much "holding" can be suffocating. A parent who is overly attached fosters fear and stifles independence, but when there is no adult to whom a child feels attached, a deep sense of loss and aloneness prevail, darkening the sky of adulthood.

Psychiatric Diagnoses

In a society grounded in male values, the need or desire for emotional closeness, central to the lives of women, has been viewed as weakness. This need, basic for all, has been assigned to women and devalued. Taught to deny their dependence on others, masculinity has masqueraded as strength, but when circumstances create feelings of helplessness, men tend to turn to anger or silent withdrawal rather than seeking comfort in relationships. Miller makes the point that as the primary caretakers of the young and the elderly, women have intimate contact with human vulnerability and thus are better to cope when tragedy strikes.

Having spent the first thirty-five years of my life desperately wanting intimacy, support, and understanding, terrified that I would overwhelm a man with my unmet needs, it was a relief to find validation in the ideas of self-in-relation theory. As I learned to see my needs as human needs, I began to value and require their acknowledgment in my relationships, especially with men.

In the newest version of the *Diagnostic and Statistical Manual of Mental Disorders* (DSM-5), the bible of psychiatrist diagnoses, the necessity for emotional engagement is reframed as "dependent personality disorder." Though eligibility for this diagnosis requires that the behavior be chronic, many of the diagnostic criteria could have applied to me before my marriage crashed. Yes, I was dependent on my husband to navigate the big, wide, scary world. Yes, I was afraid my needs were driving him away. Yes, I saw him as strong and myself as weak. Yes, I held on to my marriage for dear life. Yes, I was afraid to be alone. But these fears were based on a sea of messages directly and subtly transmitted to me by family and society and not some defect in my personality structure.

Dependent personality disorder can also be wrongly applied to women in abusive relationships. They would, according to the diagnosis, be agreeable, ingratiating, and self-deprecating. These behaviors, learned reactions and survival strategies, to avoid physical abuse, are responses to an acute situation, potentially modifiable, if and when a woman finds the courage to leave the relationship.

A popular stand-in for "dependent personality disorder" is the pseudodiagnosis of "codependency," a label originally tagged to the partners of alcoholics (usually women) who "enabled" and remained with their alcoholic mates. It wasn't long before any woman who remained in an unsatisfying relationship was labeled "codependent," pathologizing scores of women trying to maintain their intimate relationships. Both the official and pseudoofficial diagnoses ignore the impact of socialization that encourages women to be tuned into the needs of others and to blame themselves, not their partners, when their efforts fail. Perhaps these codependent women are barking up the wrong men, but it seems harsh to slap them with a diagnosis for trying. It is easy to judge a woman who stays with a partner who treats her like stale bread. Come on, I've thought; stand up for yourself. Don't let him trample on your flowerbed. Better still, leave him. I didn't say any of these things to my clients, even in mild therapeutic language, because the last thing an emotionally abused woman needs is another bully who makes her feel like a chump for staying. She may nod in agreement, but you will be met with passive resistance. More helpful is to honor her attempts to connect emotionally with her partner, as in, "I know you care about John and have tried to be close to him." If she feels that her efforts to maintain the relationship are understood and not dismissed as weak or stupid, she may be open to looking at whether her efforts have yielded the results she desires, as in, "When you try to comfort John, what happens?"

I would have liked to see all maltreated women ditch their partners. There may be "forty ways to leave your lover," but ending even a terrible relationship can be wrenching. When you think about it, whose problem is it anyway: the woman who wants emotional closeness or the partner who is unwilling or unable to engage? What if the behaviors associated with male strength were seen as psychological deficits much the same way women's behaviors have been seen as signs of pathology? Here is a psychologist, Marcie Kaplan, having a little fun with a hypothetical diagnosis viewed from a feminist and self-in-relation perspective. This is how it would appear in the *Diagnostic and Statistical Manual* (DSM), the bible of psychiatric diagnoses.

Restricted Personality Disorder:

A. Behavior that is overly restrained and unresponsive indicated by:
   1. Apparent underreaction to major events, for example, is often described as stoic.

2. Limited expression of emotions, for example, absence of crying at sad moments.

B. Disturbances in interpersonal relationships indicated by:

1. Subject changing, silence, annoyance, or leave-taking when others introduce feeling related topics.
2. Resistance to responding to others' needs by forgetting, falling asleep, or attending to other business.

Psychotherapy

From the beginning, feminist therapists had crossed the line that had demarked appropriate therapist behavior. We were more active, pushing women to question familiar beliefs, encouraging them to rekindle old aspirations, sharing our perceptions, and, when relevant, our personal experiences. Self-in-relation theory proposed that sharing our emotional reactions with our clients creates a bond of mutual understanding, the bedrock of a relationship that heals.

When the therapist and client connect emotionally, when she knows in her bones that her therapist has understood her true feelings and can reflect them back, a bond is formed. When Meg, the "male identified" woman whom I described in chapter seven, recounted without emotion the multiple abandonments studding her childhood, my response reflected the pain and sorrow I felt. Her amazement at my emotional reaction enabled her to connect with her feelings of abandonment and loss. A neutral response would have delayed an exploration of those buried feelings and might have reinforced her mask of indifference. When she saw that I had felt the pain hiding under her facile reporting of the facts, an emotional connection was created that allowed healing to begin.

I had other such moments with clients, and they were powerful and precious.

Another example occurred with Margo, the woman also mentioned in chapter seven, who was struggling to free herself from the mind-bending double bind. One day she confessed that after a date she would go back to her apartment, and sitting in her rocking chair, sip wine, listen to her favorite singer, and rock—back and forth, back and forth. She was embarrassed and worried by her need to do this. I said, "I think you are trying to soothe yourself." She looked up with an expression that said, "That's right." Then in a leap of insight, I said, "I think you are trying to return to yourself." She became solemn, and tears formed in the corners of her eyes. I had touched a painful truth. When she was with a man, she gave herself away. I said nothing, but my eyes said, "I know," and the nod of my head said, "I understand." And she knew I did.

We've all survived relationships where disconnection was the norm. The most damaging ones occur during childhood when caring is haphazard, attention minimal, and empathy scarce or nonexistent. Rather than fostering self-understanding and personal growth, these relationships do the opposite. We feel invisible, stupid, weak, and inadequate. We adapt by finding strategies, building defenses, or pretending to be someone we are not. These adaptive solutions tag along like a lost cat that sits at your back door and won't go away. They follow us into adulthood even though the circumstances that produced them are no longer present. For example, I responded to the silence surrounding my mother's death by blocking access to my grief, fear of abandonment, and need for love and comfort. I felt that acknowledging these feelings, let alone voicing them, would lead to no good. Yet, they hovered beneath the surface of my cool, seemingly self-sufficient persona. Fear of being alone and helpless, a sad refrain from a once terrified ten-year-old prevented me from taking risks. I'm sure I avoided taking a semester abroad when many of my peers grabbed the opportunity. No doubt that fear caused me to marry before I was ready to someone I wasn't sure I loved.

From a self-in-relation point of view, many of the problems people bring to therapy result from a lifetime of adapting to the multiple experiences of disconnection. The goal of therapy is to foster self-awareness and authenticity, to help clients bring more and more of their true selves to the fore. Being truly oneself feels like taking a full, deep breath and letting the air out slowly, bringing a sense of dignity and peace. In my opinion, the main avenue for achieving this is the therapeutic relationship itself.

Self-in-relation theory proved to be useful for men as well. Men often came into therapy with only one main strategy and were frustrated because they couldn't think themselves out of their confusion and depression. It's not uncommon for people, often men, to think: *If I go with my feelings, they will take over and who knows what will happen.* My response would be, "You know, attending to your feelings doesn't cause your brain to cease functioning." After the pause that usually followed, I would go on. "It makes sense to know what you're feeling. They exert influence whether you recognize them or not. Better put them in the mix. It makes for better decision-making." I would suggest that one's emotions are important sources of information and tried to offer a receptive environment for exploring and expressing them.

By valuing women's experience of the world as equal but different from that of men's, self-in-relation theory created an opening to address male and female differences without blaming either for their miscommunications. Wives tend to want their husbands to listen, empathize, and share their feelings and are hurt when they don't. Their male partners, often unschooled in the ways of female communication, can be defensive and tied to the familiar mode of rational problem solving. He: "I am trying to solve this problem." She: "But you're not listening to me. You don't understand. "Psychiatrist Dr. Stephen Bergman and psychologist Janet Surrey discuss gender differences from a self-in-relation point of view in an article, "The Woman-Man Relationship: Impasses and Possibilities." They focused on the impediments to communication between men and women that block intimacy or, in self-in-relation terms, "emotional connection."

One common stalemate: Women tend to shy away from conflict and try to find a way to resolve it by seeking a mutual resolution, while men often experience conflict as a competition, a win-lose situation. Having watched my husband and I fall into this trap, the truth of this gender difference hit home. Me: "Why are you turning this into an argument? It was only my opinion."

The first couple I saw after attending a workshop given by the authors, Bergman and Surrey, were Matt and Joan. They were stuck at every gender impasse. Identifying gender differences helped; it allowed them to view each other with less judgment and anger, even though Matt had to hang onto control. This made meeting in the middle—building avenues of communication and restoring a sense of connection—difficult. A couple of months into therapy Joan got pregnant. They were delighted and, soon after, ended therapy, which they said was very helpful. *OK.* Even the most sensible of interventions do not guarantee success. I smiled and wished them good luck.

The Therapeutic Relationship in Psychotherapy

How important is the therapeutic relationship to the outcome in psychotherapy? In traditional psychoanalytic therapy, the therapist acts as blank slate on which the patient can project his or her unconscious secrets and fears. In other theories, techniques trump the relationship. In Gestalt therapy, for example, the therapist is more of a director, using his or her sense of the patients' problems to instruct the patient in one or more of the theory's specific techniques. Though a working relationship is important in cognitive-behavioral therapy, it is the behavioral strategies that are the agents of change.

The most recent data about the therapeutic relationship comes from *Psychotherapy Relationships That Work*, a book by John Norcross. The book is a meta-analysis (a study of studies on the same topic) that investigated the association between elements in the therapeutic relationship and the effectiveness of therapy. The clear-cut conclusion was, "The therapy relationship makes substantial and consistent contributions to patient success in all types of psychotherapy studied (e.g., psychodynamic, humanistic, cognitive, behavioral, and systemic). It accounts for why clients improve (or fail to improve) as much as the particular treatment method." In another metareview published in 2002, the author asked clients what characteristics of the relationship they valued most. They named understanding, acceptance, empathy, warmth, and support. The perfect soup.

In 2012, I was reading the opinion section of the *Sunday New York Times* and found myself scanning a column by the very sane and conservative columnist, David Brooks, who writes about politics and culture. He claimed that we ignore the importance of both relationships and emotions in our policies and actions. He wrote, "We are not individuals who form relationships. We are social animals, deeply interpenetrated with one another who emerge out of relationships." *Hum.* He then went on to describe some of the relational skills required for oiling our interactions with one another. One was "attunement, the ability to enter other minds," that is, empathy. The other was "equipoise, the ability to monitor the movement of one's own mind," in other words, mutual empathy.

Self-in-relation theory blended with what I had come to see as essential: a wide-angle view of human behavior, taking into account the past, that time in life when one is a captive audience, when the experiences and relationships from childhood influence and form our sense of self. Though I was an eclectic user of techniques from other theoretical approaches, for me the most important agent of change was the therapeutic relationship.

As I write this in 2016, the essentiality of relationships is part of our cultural conversation. Advice abounds about how to communicate with spouses, children, and bosses, how to fight, how to make up, and how to talk about death.

Not long ago, I was on the train that takes you from the Thirtieth Street Station in Philadelphia to the airport. I was looking but not seeing the large advertisement directly in front of me. Then suddenly it registered, "The Relationship Center" offering counseling to individuals, couples, and groups. Relationships, it seems, are the rice and bread of life. Those rich in understanding, genuineness, caring, warmth, and especially empathy are good for infants, children, men, women, and all those who seek help in psychotherapy.

Psychotherapy

This is what I know:
Offer compassion
Always care
Practice empathy
Ponder what it's like to be another
Listen with an open heart
Refrain from judgment
Clear your mind
Banish preconceptions and bias
Be curious and watch closely
Question but don't interrogate
Do not leap but
Tread carefully
Be humble
Remember, you are a stranger in a strange land
learning its customs and myths
Support courage
Reflect sadness
Offer understanding
Learn patience
Stay grounded
Remember we all want to be *seen*
Whatever theory guides you
know that all change springs from a relationship
rich in these basic ingredients

Ten

Approaching Fifty

This is what 50 looks like.

Comment by Gloria Steinem (1997) on turning fifty

Women's liberation is celebrating its 50th anniversary, marking the formation of the first consciousness-raising groups in Chicago and New York in 1967. How to begin to enumerate the changes in women's lives that have occurred over the last fifty years? When I found the women's movement in 1969, the idea of a woman president was as improbable as a colony on Mars, but in 2016, Hilary Clinton was the democratic candidate for president of the United States. Currently, there are three women in the Supreme Court, there is a female chairman of the Federal Reserve, a serious big-boy job, and four women filled cabinet seats in President Obama's last term.

As feminism chewed away at the foundation of patriarchy, the results were obvious for all to see. In 1967, 14.8 percent of American woman were in the workforce according to the Census Bureau. In 2013, the Bureau of Labor Statistics reported that the percentage was 57.2 percent. The "daughters generation," women born from 1965 to 1983, poured into the workforce becoming doctors, lawyers, welders, legislators, mayors, entrepreneurs, and of course, artists and writers whose works, at last, found visibility. In 1971, only 7.6 percent of practicing lawyers were women. In 2016, it rose to 34 percent. In 1970, you would have had to look long and hard to find a woman physician, as only 9.7 percent of doctors were female. Today many of us, including myself, have a female physician because approximately 33 percent are women.

When I began this book in 2012, identifying oneself as a feminist was still out of style. In a 2009 CBS poll, 69 percent of women surveyed recognized that the women's movement had made their lives better, and 77 percent believed their opportunities to succeed were better than those of their mothers. Only 24 percent called themselves feminists. In that same poll Gloria Steinem, whose name is synonymous with the second wave women's movement, was unknown to 78 percent of women surveyed. Moving on to a 2016 poll commissioned by the Feminist Majority Foundation, 59 percent of women voters surveyed identified themselves as feminists. I knew that feminism was losing some of its toxicity when Beyoncé and other celebrities were calling themselves feminists. After nearly fifty years of marginalizing feminists, we seem to be at a tipping point, with feminism finding a foot in the mainstream.

The most important change has been in women's attitudes about themselves. Our daughters and now our daughter's daughters don't question their right to work, to pursue a career, or start a business. They don't wonder whether they are smart enough, capable enough, or assertive enough simply because they are female. That sense of innate inferiority that was intrinsic to society's view of women has mostly dissipated.

Feminism won the battle with psychiatry that was riddled with gender role stereotypes, causing women to feel defective if they were dissatisfied with or had rejected the traditional female role. Feminist therapy challenged the one-down position of the all-knowing psychotherapist and promoted a collaborative relationship. This allowed therapists to be more transparent about their points of view and interventions and, when relevant, their personal experiences. Self-in-relation theory emphasized the indispensability of the therapy relationship, especially salient for women, but to all therapeutic encounters that heal.

The double bind, that Gordian knot, the dichotomous and unwinnable choice between adulthood and womanhood has largely frayed and women feel freer to be both, smart and feminine. Yet it still can persist in the workplace. I recently saw a woman on TV describing her job and its requirement to be both feminine and tough. She said it was like balancing on the apex of a triangle. *Ouch!*

Another kind of double bind still pulls women, like a taut rubber band, in opposing directions; the need or desire to work versus the tug of motherhood and family. I saw working, married mothers stressed to the max, not a minute to themselves, angry at their husbands, and mumbling about separation. Their male partners, liberal in their views about women's equality, were unused to taking responsibility for tasks their mothers accomplished without complaint.

Though there have been positive changes on the housekeeping and child-caring front, a 2008 study from the University of Michigan reported that while men did more household chores, (thirteen hours per week) than they did in 1976 (seven hours per week), women were still logging in seventeen hours. In 2016, The Bureau of Labor Statistics reported that men put in one hour and twenty-five minutes on household chores, a scant twenty-five minutes more than in 1976. Women's contribution has also remained static at two hours and fifteen minutes per day. Plus, "household chores," did not include time-consuming family logistics that fall mainly on women: keeping track of who should be where when—dentist appointments, birthday parties, or parent-teacher meetings—deciding what to buy for a week for dinners, or picking up a needed winter jacket for a child on your way home from work. We have made some progress, but it seems that mothers still carry the load, and dads help out.

What is still left undone? One is the representation of women in congress. In the US Congress in 2017, 20 percent of our senators are women, and of 435 representatives in the House, only eight-eight are women. In a list ranking 190 countries on the percentage of women in their respective governing bodies, the United States is tied with Panama at seventy-two. Numbers are power.

My second long-standing grievance is the lack of childcare and parental leave. This seemingly unsolvable problem has been hanging on the clothesline, faded and torn, blowing in the wind for years. In America it's every mother for herself: costly preschool, a paid person to watch the kids, or if she is lucky, a willing family member who lives nearby. This continued to be a problem for my daughter's generation, the "Gen Xers," the first generation of women for whom affordable childcare was imperative.

Currently, France offers mothers sixteen weeks of leave with 100 percent of their wages. Sweden, in its usual top-rung position, offers 420 days at 80 percent of wages. A statistic that ramps up my ire appeared in the *Huffington Post.* An international survey found that 178 countries have paid leave for working mothers and more than fifty countries provide wage benefits for fathers. The only country with unpaid maternal leave is the United States. Oops, except for Papua New Guinea, Swaziland, Liberia, and Lesotho.

More women would "lean in," as Sheryl Sandberg urges them to do in her book of the same name if women had parental leave and affordable, quality childcare.

My third peeve is women's history or the lack of it. I admit I haven't consulted any high-school history curricula lately, but I hope that the struggle for women's equality is included. All I remember about women's suffrage from my ninth-grade history class is a photo of a frowning Susan B. Anthony, who apparently toiled single-handedly to secure the vote for women. A more sophisticated eleventh-grade American-history class ignored the women's suffrage entirely. Until I became a part of women's liberation in 1969, I knew nothing about the voices of Elizabeth Cady Stanton, Lucy Stone, and sisters Sarah and Angelia, Grimke who were born on a plantation in Charleston and became abolitionists and feminists. Women's history should be part of every high-school history curriculum, including feminism's second wave that uncovered the underlying and "nonconscious" patriarchal assumptions about women, opening the last door to true equality. Time to honor our foremothers with the same esteem we have conferred on our forefathers.

My last foray into feminist activism was a course I designed for the University of Maryland School of Social Work called Clinical Social Work Social Practice with Women. By 1998 most social-work schools had a least one course on women's issues. Maryland was coming up for accreditation and needed a course about women. I volunteered and designed a feminist-based course that I taught for four years. It was a long-desired goal to bring together twenty years of thinking about the effects of feminism on women's mental health, psychotherapy, and women's psychology.

We began with sex-role socialization and its pervasive, unconscious effects on women's lives and their mental health. We moved onto the sexist bias in clinical theories, diagnoses, and practice. I presented the origin and practice of feminist therapy and self-in-relation theory. We discussed issues for lesbians (transgender issues were not yet on the radar) and African American women who faced a double dose of discrimination. We then moved on to body image, with its crazy-making effects on women's minds and bodies, and finally to the troika of violence against women: spouse abuse, sexual assault, and child sexual abuse. In 2002, I taught the last women's class, and felt finished.

Not everyone is given the opportunity to hitch their wagons to a movement for social change. I was lucky. The time was right, and I was ready. I rode the second wave of feminism as it washed ashore and watched as it transformed every aspect of women's lives and mine.

Works Cited

Introduction

Brownmiller, Susan. 1999. *In Our Time: Memoir of a Revolution.* New York: Dell Publishing.

Chapter One Catching the Second Wave

Bem, Sandra, and Daryl Bem. 1969. "Teaching the Woman to Know Her Place: The Power of the Nonconscious Ideology." *Women: A Journal of Liberation.*

Hanisch, Carol. 1970. "The Personal Is Political." In *Notes from the Second Year: Women's Liberation,* edited by Shulamith Firestone.

Chapter Two The Double Bind

Bateson G. D., J. Jackson, J. Haley, and J. Weakland. 1956. "Toward a Theory of Schizophrenia." *Behavioral Science* 1:251–54.

Broverman, I. K., D. M. Broverman, F. E. Clarkson, F. S. Rosenkrantz, and S. R. Vogel. 1970. "Sex-role Stereotypes and Clinical Judgment of Mental Health." *Journal of Consulting and Clinical Psychology* 34:1–7.

Miller, Jean Baker. 1976. *Toward a New Psychology of Women.* Boston: Beacon Press.

Pancoast, Ruth, and Westin, Linda 1974. "Feminist Psychotherapy: A Method for Fighting the Social Control of Women." Paper presented at the American Orthopsychiatry Association Meeting, San Francisco, CA.

Chapter Three Motherless Daughters

Edelman, Hope. 2006. *Motherless Daughters.* Philadelphia, PA: Da Capo Press.

Chapter Four Body Politics

Boston Women's Health Collective. 1972. *Our Bodies Ourselves.* Boston: New England Free Press.

Chicago Tribune. March, 2017. "Media, Diversity, and Social Change Initiative." University of Southern California, Annanburg School for Communication and Journalism.

Klos, Diana Mitsu. "The Status of Women in the US Media 2013." Women's Media Center. women'smediadentercom

Masters, W., and V. Johnson. 1966. *Human Sexual Response.* New York: ISHO Press.

Stone, Lucy. 1985. "25 Quotes by Lucy Stone." AZ Quotes.com.

Steinam, Gloria (1993) Revolution from the Inside Out: A Book of Self-Esteem. New Y York:Little Brown

Woolf, Naomi. 1991. *Hunger, The Beauty Myth.* New York: William Morrow.

United States Census Bureau, May, 2015. https://www.census.gov/newsroom/facts-for-features/2015/cb15-ff09.html. https://www.census.gov

Chapter Five Getting to the Starting Gate

Castenado, Carlos. http://www.azquotes.com/author/2613-Carlos_Castaneda?p=6

Deutsch, H. 1944. *The Psychology of Women.* New York: Grune and Stratton.

Chapter Six Women Counselling Women

Chesler, Phyliss. 1972. *Women and Madness.* New York: Doubleday.

Greenspan, M. 1993. *A New Approach to Women & Therapy.* 2nd ed. Blue Ridge Summit, PA: Tab Books.

Heriot, Jessica. 1983. "The Double Bind: Healing the Split." In *Women Changing Therapy: New Assessments, Values, and Strategies in Feminist Therapy,* edited by J. H. Robbins and R. J. Siegel. New York: Haworth Press. P.11

Lerner, Harriet. 1974. "The Early Origins of Envy and the Devaluation of Women: A Critique of Freudian Theory." *Bulletin of the Menninger Clinic.*38:538

Miller, Jean Baker. 1972. "Psychological Consequences of Sexual Inequality." *American Journal of Psychiatry* 32: 147.

Pancoast, Ruth, and Weston, Linda. 1974. "Feminist Psychotherapy: A Method for Fighting the Social Control of Women." Paper presented at the American Orthopsychiatry Association, San Francisco, CA.

Taylor, Anne. 2002. "Mad Colored Women: A Memoir of Manic Depression." In *Personal Narratives in the Helping Professions: A Teaching Casebook,* edited by J. Heriot and E. Pollinger. New York: Haworth Press: 225.

Weisstein, Naomi. 1970. "Kinder, Kuche, Kirche as Scientific Law: Psychology Constructs the Female." In *Sisterhood Is Powerful,* edited by R. Morgan. New York: Vintage Press: page number unavailable

Chapter Seven Practicing Feminist Therapy

Brown, Laura (1994) *Subversive Dialogues: Theory in Feminist Therapy*. New York: Basic Books.

Gladwell, Malcom. 2008. *Outliers*. New York: Little Brown.

Chapter Eight Incest: The Last Box

Elliott, Ann N., and Carnes Connie N. 2001. "Reactions of Non-offending Parents to the Sexual Abuse of Their Children: A Review of the Literature." *Child Abuse and Neglect* 6 (4): 314–31.

Heriot, Jessica. 1996. "Maternal Protectiveness Following the Disclosure of Intrafamilial Child Sexual Abuse." *Journal of Interpersonal Violence* 11.181

Herman, Judith. 1981. *Father Daughter Incest.* Cambridge, MA: Harvard University Press.

Herman, Judith. 1992. *Trauma and Recovery: The Aftermath of Violence from Domestic Abuse to Political Terror.* New York: Basic Books.

Zuravin, Susan, and Denise Pintello. 2001. "Intra-familial Child Sexual Abuse: Predictors of Post-disclosure Maternal Belief and Protective Action." *Child Maltreatment* 6 (4):344.

Chapter Nine Finding A Therapeutic Home

Ardito, R. B., and A. D. Rabellion. 2011."Therapeutic Alliance and Outcome of Psychotherapy: Historical Excursus, Measurements, and Prospects for Research." *Frontiers in Psychology* 2:270.

Bergman, S., and J. Surrey. 1992. *The Woman-man Relationship: Impasses and Possibilities.* Work in Progress no. 55. Wellesley, MA: Stone Center.

Brooks, D. "The New Humanism." *New York Times OP-ED.* March 8th, 2011.

Erikson, E. 1968. *Identity Youth and Crisis.* New York: WW Norton.

Gilligan, Carol. 1982. *In a Different Voice: Psychological Theory and Women's Development.* Cambridge, MA: Harvard University Press.

Josselson, R. E. 1992. *The Space between Us: Exploring the Dimensions of Human Relationships.* San Francisco: Jossey-Bass Inc.

Kaplan, M. 1983. "A Women's View of DSM111." *American Psychologist* 38:786–92.

Lambert, J. D., and E. Barley. 2002. "Research Summary on the Therapeutic Relationship and Psychotherapy Outcomes." *Psychotherapy: Theory, Research, Practice and Training* 38 (4). Could not find page #

Lerner, Harriet. 1974. "Early Origins of Envy and Devaluation of Women: Implications for Sex-Role Stereotypes. *Bulletin of the Menniger Clinic.38. 538.*

Levinson, D. (1998) *The Seasons of a Man's Life.* New York: Barnes and Noble.

Miller, J. B. 1986. *What Do We Mean by Relationships?* (Work in Progress #22). Wellesley, MA: Stone Center.

Miller, J. B., and I. Stiver. 1991. "Relational Reframing of Therapy." Paper presented at Stone Center Colloquium Series. Wellesley, MA.

Norcross, J. 2002. *Psychotherapy Relationships that Work: Evidence-based Responsiveness.* New York: Oxford University Press.

Perlman, H. H. 1979. *Relationship: The Heart of Helping People.* Chicago: University of Chicago Press.

Rogers, C. 1975. "Empathetic: An Unappreciated Way of Being." *The Counseling Psychologist* 5 (2):210.

Stern, D. 1986. *The Interpersonal World of the Infant.* New York: Basic Books.

Turner, F. 1996. *Social Work Treatment.* 4th ed. New York: The Free Press.

Chapter Ten Approaching Fifty

American Bar Association. 2013. "Current Glance at Women in Law." *Commission on Women in the Profession.* https://www.americanbar.org

Sean Alfono. "Poll Women's Movement Worthwhile" *CBS News.* 2009. www.cbsnews.com/news/poll-womens-movement-worthwhile.

Druckerman, Pamela. "Catching Up with France on Day Care." *New York Times,* September 1st. 2013.

Freedman, Jessica. 2016. "Women in Medicine: Are We Here Yet?" www.medscape.com. 26

Inter-Parlimentry Union. "Women in National Parliaments." July 1st 2017. www.ipu.org/wmn-e/world.htm.

Marche, S. 2013. "The Case for Filth: Young Men Are Doing No More Housework than Their Fathers Did." *New York Times,* December.8th.

Adams Rebecda."Parental Leave: US vs. the World." 2015. *Huffington Post.* January 14th www.huffingtonpost.com 2015/01/14/parental-leave-around-the-world_n_6464910.html.

PRWeb. 2017. "Report from AMA physician list." www.prweb.com

Sandberg, S. 2013. *Lean in: Women, Work, and the Will to Lead.* New York: Alfred Knopf.

Smeal, Eleanor. 2016. "Beyond the Gender Gap: Growing the Feminist Factor." *MS*, Winter. 27

Stafford Frank "Exactly How Much Housework Does a Husband Create?" *IRS /sampler.* Summer 2008 *Vol 7 (1).* www. mich.edu/news/families/

US Bureau of Labor Statistics. 2013. http://www.bls.gov

About the Author

Jessica Heriot, PhD, is a retired psychotherapist and passionate feminist. She has a doctorate in social work and worked as an adjunct professor at the University of Maryland School of Social Work. During her thirty-two years as a psychotherapist, Heriot worked mainly with women. She helped found a feminist counseling center in Baltimore and coedited the book *The Uses of Personal Narratives in the Helping Profession: A Teaching Casebook.*

Heriot's dissertation on intrafamilial child sex abuse was published in *The Journal of Interpersonal Violence.* She has also published several poems and short stories.

Heriot currently lives with her husband in Hendersonville, North Carolina.